Jessica Kingsley *Publishers*
London and Philadelphia

First published in 2018

by Jessica Kingsley Publishers
73 Collier Street
London N1 9BE, UK
and
400 Market Street, Suite 400
Philadelphia, PA 19106, USA

www.jkp.com

Library of Congress Cataloging in Publication Data
A CIP catalog record for this book is available from the Library of Congress

British Library Cataloguing in Publication Data
A CIP catalogue record for this book is available from the British Library

ISBN 978 1 78592 229 9
eISBN 978 1 78450 504 2

Printed and bound in Great Britain

To the 'unsung heroes': all the hard working, dedicated local authority workers out there. Here's to less blame and more praise and encouragement for the amazing work you do.

Acknowledgements

Special thanks to my husband Gwyn for his support and advice, for reading the very first draft, for pointing out some of my very 'clunky' sentences and reminding me about full stops.

Thanks also to my sister, Janet Benwell, and ex-colleague Sarah-Jane Hopkins for reading my final draft. I really appreciated their enthusiasm, their encouragement, their helpful suggestions and positive feedback.

Finally I am grateful to Gillian Thrower and Margaret Phelps, and to the numerous other colleagues I have had the privilege of working alongside. They have inspired and supported me throughout my social work career.

These are just some of the many 'unsung heroes'.

Contents

1. Introduction   7

2. Life Work Terminology   11

3. Purpose of Life Work   14

4. The Theoretical Framework   17

5. The Team Around the Child   33

6. Aspects of Life Work   47

7. Summing Up   83

Appendix A   *85*

Appendix B   *96*

Appendix C   *98*

Appendix D   *100*

References   *115*

Suggested reading   *117*

Children's books   *119*

Introduction

This book explores the purpose and different aspects of life work with children who are fostered and adopted. It is written drawing on my experience of working within a local authority children's service.

As a social work practitioner, manager and trainer, I have worked directly and indirectly with children in care throughout my career. Most of these children were living with, or about to move to, permanent substitute families. Many were placed years prior to my involvement, and it was with the benefit of hindsight that I began to reflect on the purpose of life work and the effect that this had on the children I met.

I was particularly concerned about the adverse impact, and the poor quality, of some of the life story books I read. Many were confusing and not child-centred. I began to compile these books in a different way and with a different emphasis. My focus was on making them more child-friendly, raising the child's self-esteem and promoting a sense of security and belonging within their permanent family. This led to the publication of *Life Story Books for Adopted Children* and, the updated version, *Life Story Books for Adopted and Fostered Children* (Rees 2009, 2017).

Over the last decade, I have had the opportunity of sharing my approach with adoptive parents, foster carers and social care providers throughout the UK. It is gratifying to know that 'the Rees model',[1] with the present – past – present – future format, has been widely embraced by local authorities. However, from recent experiences of working with some agencies, it is clear that many professionals are still confused about the wider concept of life work. Like the children they are trying to serve, some have their own 'why, what, how and when' questions (Ryan and Walker 2016), in relation to this aspect of the work.

The significance of life work is universally acknowledged. There is a general consensus that, fundamentally, it's about helping children to understand their histories and giving them a sense of identity. However, the quality and quantity of this work varies considerably between local authorities. Some give it high priority and see it as an integral part of the social work brief; they employ staff to specialize in this area of the work and have built up considerable expertise and resources. Others do minimal life work with the children in their care; they have an insular approach and regard it as an extra task, done in a last minute rush, for example, when the child is moving to a permanent placement. Some practitioners see it as a very skilled area of work: something to be provided by an external 'therapeutic service', especially when the child's behaviour has become particularly worrying or challenging.

Life work should lie at the very heart of our involvement with all children in care. But, for some reason, it seems that 'not enough of this vital work takes place' (Wrench and Naylor 2013, p.9). Indeed, in some children's services, little has changed since

---

1   This model gently and playfully engages the child. By starting in the present, the book reinforces the child's sense of security, before exploring past trauma. It ends with hope for a positive future.

Nicholls noted 'the demise in any meaningful life work', and her observation that it had 'become an afterthought, something that had to be done only when a child was at the point of moving on to permanence' (Nicholls 2005, p.xi). Similarly, Baynes observed that life work had become 'a peripheral task'…'seen as an optional extra rather than as a core social work skill'. (Baynes 2008, p.44).

Too many competing demands and lack of time are considered the main obstacles preventing social care practitioners undertaking this 'vital work'. They cite austerity measures, tighter timescales, increased targets and reduced staffing as the principal problems. Others feel the emphasis on evidence-based practice and providing supporting data depletes the time practitioners have to spend actually interacting with children. Some allude to 'tick box exercises' and 'number games' and feel the proscriptive policies limit the scope for innovation, and for the creative and playful activities associated with life work.

The difficulties are undeniable and, while the challenges facing social care providers are plainly evident, the lack of life work may not only be attributed to 'too much work, too little time'. Other factors include:

- **Training and guidance.** It seems that life work is not an area that is covered in any depth – and in some instances not at all – on social work training courses. This gap in knowledge may be further compounded by the absence of clear departmental procedures and policies, and the lack of easily-available practical resources. These deficiencies lead to misconceptions about the nature and purpose of life work. Further misunderstanding causes delays in starting, and disagreements about who should do this work and when.

- **The emphasis on performance indicator-led practice.** The very nature of life work makes measuring the quality and quantity difficult. The number of sessions undertaken with a child can be recorded, but this in itself is not an indication of the quality or effectiveness of this contact. A completed life story book may be a good indicator that some direct work has been done with the child, but this may not be the case. There is a danger of misinterpretation if inspecting life work out of context. 'A pile of messy drawings may represent a piece of high quality, deeply personal work with a child, while a beautifully presented book may have little or no meaning for the child' (Baynes 2008, p.45).

- **Life work is an ongoing and lifelong process and will be revisited many times.** It is not one piece of work that can be ticked off. It is never *done*, so 'it is difficult to inspect and defies organisational timescales' (Baynes 2008, p.45).

- **Failure to appreciate the different aspects of life work.** Many professionals think of life work only as the direct work involving the child, or the life story book, as this is something that is tangible. Life work is multidimensional. There are many other important aspects and they do not all involve the child directly. Furthermore, life work with the child can be informal as well as formal. There is a team around the child. Different members of this team may undertake very skilled and sensitive life work with the child in a relaxed, spontaneous, informal way. This element is not always recognized or recorded as such.

- **Confusion about current terminology.** Some practitioners and managers are simply puzzled by the many terms used: life work, life story work, life journey work, direct work, life books, life story books, memory books and boxes, etc. Exploration of these terms may be a useful place to begin.

Note: I refer to 'children' throughout this book. It is an inclusive term and also represents young people in care.

CHAPTER 1

Life Work Terminology

The terminology is confusing and some clarification may help. Many local authorities now consider *life work* to be the most appropriate term. It is the overarching name and incorporates all of the other aspects.

Life journey work, also called *life story work*, refers to *direct work* with the child. This aspect is all about answering those 'why, what, how and when' questions children may have about their early experiences. Depending on the child's level of maturation, interests and abilities, a variety of approaches can be used to help them to understand and process their history: 'listening, talking, drawing, painting, playing, storytelling, compiling ecomaps, family trees or other diagrams, or using sand trays, puppets and interactive packages' (Rees 2017, p.19). Life journey work always involves the child.

Some practitioners favour the term life journey work rather than life story work. They feel that *story* may lead the child to wonder if the information being shared is 'true or just a tale' (Nicholls 2005, p.13). Using the same rationale, some professionals now refer to *life books*, or *life journey books*, rather than *life story books*. However, the book is literally the child's story: it is the narrative of the child's life, so *life story book* feels apt.

The *life story book* should be written in a simple, truthful and child-friendly way. A clear and honest account of the early experiences will allow the story to be told and retold. Over time, this enables the child to revisit and reinterpret their story. The child may reframe events or expand their understanding of the details as they mature. There will be opportunities to acknowledge the different perspectives (e.g. those of the birth family, social worker, foster carer, adopter and judge). This does not mean that the original life story book is untrue.

The child's book is generally regarded as the end product of life journey work although, in effect, there is no end to this work. The book should be regarded as an aid to continuing life work; or, if provided for a baby or very young child, it will be the foundation for future life work.

Unlike life journey work, the child may not be directly involved in compiling the life story book. A few children may want to write their own story, but this is unusual. Others will contribute and, if it is the culmination of life journey work, they may be more involved. Some children 'play a role in the creation…rather than be passive observers' (Rose and Philpot 2005, p. 120). Ultimately, pulling all the information together and creating the book is still the responsibility of 'the worker and not the child' (Rose and Philpot 2005, p.128).

The foster carer, with the support and guidance of the child's social worker and fostering supervising worker, should gather memorabilia (e.g. trinkets, certificates, special gifts, photographs, etc.) for the child's *memory box*. They should also compile a *memory book* to capture and record details the child's life and experiences while living with them. Foster carers should not be expected to compile life story books for children in their care. This is not their responsibility, but they should contribute to the book.

Children may be reluctant to begin life *work*. They have school*work* and home*work*, so understandably more *work* is not appealing. Perhaps, particularly when engaging younger children, we should avoid all social work jargon. An *All About Me* book or, possibly, *life play* may be more fitting and more appealing concepts. Although this work entails processing sad and difficult information, it also involves playful activities and there is usually fun and laughter along the way. The ability to be playful is required in all our communications with children. Wrench and Taylor also note that some of the children they worked with later recalled that life work helped them to 'understand something of their history', and they also remembered 'the fun they had' (Wrench and Naylor 2013, p. 22)

Social work jargon will continue to evolve. Whatever terms are used now or in the future, it is an understanding of purpose and an appreciation of the different aspects that may be the key to raising the profile, the quantity and quality of life work with children.

CHAPTER 2

Purpose of Life Work

The fundamental purpose of life work with all children in care is to help them to understand their history and to gain a sense of their identity. In theory, this is a clear and simple task. In reality, life work is a complex, multilayered and lifelong process.

Life work aims to help children understand why they are not able to live with their birth families and provide answers to their many – often unspoken – questions about their past and their future, such as: *What happened to me and when? Where is my birth family now? Did I do something wrong? Where have I lived? Who looked after me? Why and when were certain decisions made about my care? Can I stay here?*

With more understanding and knowledge, it is hoped that children will be able to live more comfortably in the present, and move on to enjoy a positive future. As Fahlberg and many of her contemporaries observed, 'it is difficult to grow up as a psychologically healthy adult if one is denied access to one's own history' (Fahlberg 2003, pp.353–354). She expands on the purpose of direct work:

- gaining an understanding of the child's perception of his/her life

- disengagement work

- explaining plans for the future

- addressing current areas of concern

- enhancing attachments in the current family

- facilitating identity formation

- increasing the child's knowledge of self

- reintegration of early life events

- focusing on lifelong issues (Fahlberg 2003, p.326).

Similarly, the purpose of life story books is to provide an account of the child's history and to give a sense of identity (Rees 2017, p.14), but again there are multiple aims:

- to enable the child to share their past with their adopters, carers and others

- to give a realistic account of early events and to dispel fantasies about the birth family

- to link the past to the present and to help the child, the adopter and carer to understand how earlier life events continue to impact on behaviour

- to acknowledge issues of separation and loss

- to enable adoptive parents and carers to understand and develop empathy for the child

- to enhance the child's self-esteem and self-worth

- to promote attunement and attachment.

- to help the child to develop a sense of security and permanency.

These lists overlap and they apply to all life work. They highlight the extensive benefits for children when life work is undertaken with care and sensitivity, and advise of the potential damage caused when not done.

In all children's social care interventions, the priority is to understand the child. A good grasp of the underpinning theories and of their interrelationship is vital.

CHAPTER 3

The Theoretical Framework

All of our work with children in care must be undertaken with a thorough knowledge of child development, including brain development, attachment theory and developmental trauma.

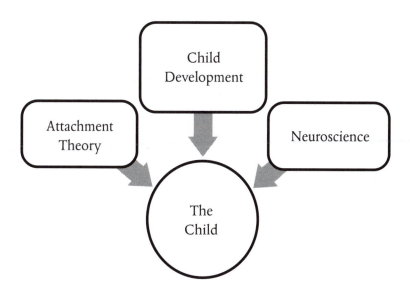

Figure 3.1: Theoretical Framework

Child development

Every child progresses through the stages of maturation in their own unique way and at their own pace. 'Normal' developmental progress suggests that functioning abilities match chronological age. There is a clear sequencing of developmental milestones. A specific stage is therefore distinguished by certain physical, psychological and emotional characteristics.

Life work is undertaken within this developmental framework, so it is helpful to consider some general guidelines. However, when thinking about the timing and most appropriate form of life work, we must always take into account the child's experiences and their emotional and cognitive development, rather than their chronological age. 'Think toddler' is the mantra of many who specialize in this area of work, as 'many of the adolescents we work with are still small inside' (Wrench and Naylor 2013, p.13).

Summary of developmental stages

Pre-birth

Within a few weeks of conception, the placenta is formed and is responsible for ensuring that the developing embryo receives oxygen and nutrients from the mother. The baby's environment, the mother's experiences and the care she takes of herself will all affect development.

> If exposed to high levels of alcohol in the womb, the child may to be born with foetal alcohol syndrome disorder (FASD). The alcohol passes easily through the placenta and this interferes with brain development and damages the nervous system. This is diagnosed at birth with some babies. If the mother drank during the first trimester, when facial features are formed, the baby may have the features associated with this syndrome – small wide set eyes, flat philtrum, thin upper lip. For others the damage is not immediately apparent and the child may be

diagnosed with this syndrome at a much later stage. Symptoms may include poor concentration, learning difficulties and challenging behaviour.

Mothers with a drug dependency may give birth to babies with an addiction. These babies tend to have a low birth weight, experience feeding difficulties and may be born in pain. They will need special care and medication to ease their discomfort and to wean them off these drugs. They are often described as 'very jittery' babies or as having 'stiff jerky movements'.

The mother's emotional state during the pregnancy can also affect the developing foetus. If mother has experienced heightened stress levels, for instance due to domestic violence, the baby may be born with high levels of the stress hormone cortisol. This can also interfere with and damage brain development.

Pre-birth experiences clearly have a huge impact on the child's potential and on their future development but, whatever their experience, babies are already in an attachment relationship. By the seventh month the foetus can open his/her eyes, see and hear. At birth, a baby is able to recognize the sounds and smell of the birth mother. While separation at this early stage, or shortly after, may be necessary, it will have a negative impact on the child. The sense of loss and trauma experienced by a newborn has been described as 'the primal wound'.

(Verrier 2009)

BIRTH TO ONE YEAR

Babies change and grow rapidly, mentally and physically during this period. Through positive everyday interaction and nurturing experiences, feelings of safety, security and trust develop. They learn to hold their head up, to roll over, to sit, to stand and then to walk. Their fine motor skills also develop and they can pick up and hold small objects. They begin to vocalize, imitate sounds and recognize their name.

By nine months they distinguish a familiar face from others. 'Stranger anxiety' develops. They seek out and feel safe if the primary attachment figure is present.

For the child who is separated from the birth parent during this period, the primary task for substitute carers is to provide safe, consistent, reliable care and nurturing, loving experiences.

ONE TO THREE YEARS

Major and fine motor skills continue to develop rapidly throughout this stage. Toddlers learn to hold a spoon and feed themselves. It's a time to explore their environment as they become physically more confident. They learn to climb and run. They start to recognize bodily sensations, so toilet training can begin, and this is usually complete by end of this period. The toddler is generally very sociable, if in a secure setting and when the main attachment figure is near. They are apprehensive about being separated from the carer. They like to remain close.

By two years they can carry an image of the carer in their head. They no longer have to be in the same room to know that he/she still exists. They begin to develop a sense of themselves as a separate being, and with this comes more oppositional behaviour. We have the 'terrible twos' as the toddler's mood swings from being helpful to being very stubborn. They alternate between being dependent and self-contained. Language skills improve but they do not have the vocabulary yet to express their feelings and frustrations verbally. They do so in their behaviour – hence the tantrums.

By the age of three years, there is plenty of imaginary play. They play alone or alongside other children, rather than with them. They haven't yet developed a sense of sharing, and tend to be very self-centred. A sense of pride and shame begins, as does a sense of good versus bad.

The right brain – full of emotions and imagery – dominates, and the connection with the left side responsible for language and logical thinking is not fully formed. Although there is a great spurt in language acquisition at this stage, and children now use phrases and sentences, they still struggle to connect feelings to words.

At this age, children live in the moment. They have limited understanding of time and concepts like yesterday, tomorrow, next week, past or future. We need to be realistic and mindful of this in relation to life work. Toddlers need simple explanations. Some play-based work can be undertaken, but the main task is still to meet their primary needs. Carers must try to minimize trauma and the effects of separation and loss by providing reassurance, consistency, predictability, and a safe, nurturing environment.

FOUR TO SEVEN YEARS

During this stage, more emotional and physical control is achieved. Children are better able to regulate their emotions, to calm themselves and self-soothe. At the beginning of this period they are generally happy and contented. They are better able to express themselves and can negotiate, so they are not so easily frustrated. They now play with other children and can take turns. They ask numerous 'how' and 'why' questions and often repeat the same questions. They are inquisitive, and are also checking and looking for consistencies in answers.

This is often referred to as the concrete, magical thinking and egocentric stage. Children like facts and believe that their wishes can make things happen. They tend to hold themselves responsible for everything that happens to them or to others in their lives. There is limited capacity to change their thinking on this, at this stage in their development.

Around the age of four or five years some children acquire an imaginary friend who can take the blame for any transgression. He/she can be the child's representative, expressing any fears or worries (e.g. the friend has eaten the cake or needs the light on at night). Fear of the dark, and asking the adult to check in the wardrobe or under the bed, is the most common fear during this stage. Being frightened of thunder and other loud noises, like sirens or dogs barking, is also common.

Most of the anxieties are still related to being separated from their main attachment figures. The underlying issue for children with school phobia, for instance, is frequently separation anxiety. They worry that something 'bad' may happen to the adult while they are apart, rather than having difficulties at school.

The child's internal sense of shame can increase at this stage. A six- or seven-year-old responds to praise better than to other forms of discipline. They are generally not good at completing 'jobs' on their own and are far more cooperative when tasks are shared. Lots of repetition and reminders are still needed. Children may regress around this age, become frustrated very easily and temper tantrums may return. Shouting, name-calling and aggression are not uncommon.

Children's feelings and thoughts are still reflected in their play rather than in their words. This can be a very productive time to use play-based life work techniques. They do not carry the emotional 'baggage' that older children and adults have. They can hear basic facts and difficult details, more easily than later on. They have an accepting, 'matter of fact' or inquisitive attitude to things that adults may find difficult or upsetting to discuss (e.g. mental health disorders or death).

Towards the end of this period children become much calmer. There is less shouting and aggression and more verbal protests of 'it's not fair!' and retreating into sulks. They are able to concentrate for longer stretches of time and become absorbed in activities.

They ignore interruptions as they become completely engrossed (e.g. watching a favourite television programme). They don't hear the adult calling them. They are not deliberately 'being naughty' and 'just ignoring'. Learning to focus and being able to screen out other distractions is an important ability to acquire. It is something that children who develop attention deficits or disorders have not mastered.

The 'good versus bad' scenario continues to be played out in their games. These concepts still tend to be extremes, with no middle ground. Someone is all good or all bad. In life work, care is needed to avoid feeding the child's sense of self-blame and shame and of being 'the baddy' in his/her own life story. If concerns about inadequate parenting are minimized, for the child the birth parents must then be 'the goodies'. This propounds the belief that any abuse or neglect suffered was the child's fault.

Children need to reflect on and reframe the information shared with them many times as they develop, and as their level of understanding increases, but this is a prime time to give a simple and truthful account: to lay a strong foundation.

Eight to ten years

At this age, the child's family still provides the secure base. This enables the child to explore and widen his/her horizons, to have adventures and to master situations outside the home. Gross motor skills improve and intellectual and reasoning abilities expand. The child is more independent and generally more responsible and cooperative. If reprimanded by a parent or carer, they are more likely to feel hurt or embarrassed rather than annoyed. Although they may be verbally abusive, they are seldom physically aggressive.

A sense of right and wrong is more established. The child's conscience develops and he/she now modifies behaviour and actions, by using internal controls rather than relying on the external ones imposed by adults. The child moves through the more egocentric stages and begins to see the world from other perspectives. A sense of empathy and feelings of guilt (as distinct from shame) develop.

Family relationships are still important to this age group but, towards the end of this stage, friendships are increasingly significant. Peer group values and beliefs can influence the child more than family values.

Brodzinsky and Schechter (1990) notes a considerable leap in cognitive abilities around this age. Greater understanding makes this stage of development particularly significant for adopted children. He suggested that many of the difficulties children experience at this time are 'unrecognized manifestations of an adaptive grieving process' (Brodzinsky and Schechter 1990, p.7). The child now has a clearer appreciation of what adoption actually means. With this comes a greater sense of the separations and losses experienced earlier.

Adoptive parents often notice their children become more subdued and withdrawn, or more challenging and angry around this age. The child is working through the classic stages for grief for the losses they experienced at a younger age. It may be a good time to revisit their life story.

Many children in long-term care have experienced multiple placements, and will go through similar phases, as they too grieve for the separations and loss of birth family and previous foster carers.

An understanding of the relationship between past and present is now emerging. The child begins to think more about their future and what they would like to achieve. Children of this age tend to show more interest in their history. They like to look at photographs of themselves when younger, and to hear stories and anecdotes about their exploits.

A sensitively written life story book, can now be used with great effect to revisit and reframe some of their early experiences. As the child's level of understanding is increasing and their ability to empathize is developing, the detail of the child's story can be expanded verbally and different perspectives gently explored. Further direct life work can be extremely productive at this stage of development.

ADOLESCENCE

Although the term 'adolescence' is usually equated with the teenage years, the physical, intellectual and psychological maturation associated with this period actually starts pre-teens and continues into early adulthood. It is a time of transition from being a child to being an adult, and all this entails: expectations of being independent; being responsible for one's own actions, able to reason, to think logically, to develop more flexibility of thinking and able to form and maintain meaningful friendships.

Adolescents experience the whole gamut of emotions – happy, angry, sad, fearful, anxious, excited – as do younger children, but in a particularly intense way. Psychologically, this stage – particularly the middle years – is similar to the toddler stage. Control issues re-emerge and teens are once again more egocentric. They see their own needs as paramount. They tend to be moody and fluctuate between being pleasant, helpful and dependable, and being grumpy, obstructive and unreliable. They strive for individuality and independence, but they also need to maintain an emotional connection to the secure base: their family and home. They still want to belong, but may also be very rebellious, while being very compliant in relation to their peer group.

Oppositional behaviour is an important part of the adolescent's development, as they try to exert some control over their lives. They need to feel that adults don't always approve of their behaviour, clothes, choice of music, state of their bedroom, etc. It gives them something to complain about and rebel against. This can have a very positive function, as it 'meets the adolescent's need for individualisation without him or her having to resort to drugs, alcohol abuse, or sex as ways of demonstrating behaviourally that adults cannot control all areas of an adolescent's development' (Fahlberg 2003, p. 109).

There is now a surge in identity formation, as the adolescent struggles to integrate different aspects of this: current family identity, and religious, ethnic, cultural and peer identity. For children who are fostered or adopted there is also the birth family and genetic identity.

Life work can help adolescents reflect on their early history and consider the impact that this has had, and is still having, on their inner beliefs and current behaviour. It can help them to understand and explain themselves to themselves, and this may enable them to feel more in control of their life path. This stage and process continues into adulthood.

This provides only a brief guide to the stages of development. Life work must be undertaken within this context, but for many children in care or adopted their development has been disrupted. Their chronological and developmental ages may not match, and they take longer to reach certain milestones. They may be described as 'developmentally delayed'. This can be in a specific area (e.g. speech or walking) or there may be 'global delay'. The latter implies significant delays in many areas like language, fine and motor skills, and in social and emotional interactions with others.

Genetics and nature play a part in determining a child's developmental progress. There is also a plethora of research showing that the environment and the quality of care the child receives, pre-birth and in their early months and years, has a profound effect on development in the short and long term. There is a general consensus that whether or not children reach their potential, whatever this may be, is affected by their early interaction with others and the quality of the care received.

Attachment theory

An experience of poverty, neglect or abuse has a negative impact on the child's growth; physically, emotionally and cognitively. Bowlby (1992), considered to be the father of attachment theory, was the first to identify the importance of 'the secure base' (Bowlby 1992, p.11). He established that the quality of the first adult relationship directly affects a child's psychological growth and development. The type of care received leads to the formation of a secure or insecure pattern of attachment.

When the first adult relationship is loving and provides reliable and consistent care, the child develops inner confidence and trust. From this safe, secure base, he/she is able to explore the world. If this first attachment figure does not provide these positive, nurturing experiences, the result will be a lack of self-worth and a mistrust of adults. The world is perceived as unsafe and the child is insecurely attached.

Further researchers and scholars (e.g. Mary Ainsworth, Mary Main, Patricia Crittenden and David Howe) demonstrated that insecurely attached children can be further divided into many different categories, but three broad groups are identified: *avoidant, ambivalent* and *disorganized* attachments. Children at the extreme may be described as disordered.

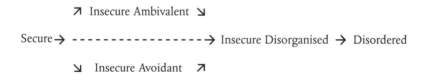

Figure 4. 2: The Attachment Continuum

Children in the insecure groups have some common characteristics. They have negative internal working models, and tend to blame themselves for the poor parenting or any abuse they have received.

Most tend to have low self-esteem and an innate sense of 'badness' and shame. They believe that any negative early experience must have been their fault.

Children in the different groups develop different coping strategies to survive in their birth families. If largely ignored, or if the child becomes aware that any bid for attention causes the adult agitation and irritation, an avoidant attachment develops. The child learns that it is best not to trouble the adult. An avoidant child may close down emotionally and become self-sufficient. They are often described as having 'built a brick wall' around themselves. They may reject intimacy and find it difficult to accept affection or nurturing. The avoidant child will not seek out an adult for help or comfort when hurt, emotionally or physically.

In contrast, the ambivalent child may stay very close to the adult carer. This child has experienced the primary attachment figure as unpredictable and inconsistent. The adult is sometimes loving and attentive, at other times dismissive, cross and preoccupied with his/her own needs. They can present as easy, smiley, compliant children. They crave approval and affection and are often described as 'overly clingy'. They can, however, alternate between being controlling and bossy, and very anxious and needy. They can be particularly vulnerable, as they tend to be indiscriminate, and will seek comfort and affection from any available adult.

The child with a disorganized attachment may employ similar coping tactics to the other groups, but the behaviour is more unpredictable and more extreme. These children will use strategies that reflect the confusing, chaotic, unpredictable, frightening and sometimes terrifying parenting they have experienced.

Whatever the insecure attachment style, to varying degrees these children will all tend to lack inner confidence, have low self-esteem and find it difficult to trust adults. Their world, in general, feels like not a very comfortable or safe place.

When considering appropriate life work techniques, practitioners must be mindful of the child's attachment style, their inner beliefs and their coping strategies.

Developments in neuroscience

Increased understanding of how the brain works reinforces the validity of attachment theory, and the importance of those early interactions on the child's development. Advances in technology and brain scans now enable neuroscientists to literally see the impact that negative experiences can have. They confirm that optimum development of the human brain relies on positive interaction and experiences with others. How children are treated affects brain development and how resourceful they become.

Brain development begins a few weeks after conception and, as noted, pre-birth experiences can adversely affect its growth. The brain continues to develop at an amazing rate in the early years of life, and during this time it is particularly responsive to external stimuli. While 'genes provide a blueprint for the brain…a child's environment and experiences carry out the construction' (The Urban Child Institute 2017). The brain's ability to shape itself, known as plasticity, and the process of 'blooming and pruning' begins. Blooming refers to the strong connections made between the neurons in the brain. These connections are strengthened the more they are used: this is blooming. Conversely, if not used or not needed, they are weeded out: this is pruning. These processes are governed by the child's experiences and continue throughout childhood, during the teenage years and into early adulthood.

The implications of this are very positive in relation to the potential impact that life work and therapeutic re-parenting techniques can have. Although early negative experiences may have negative consequences, the brain remains 'plastic', so open to change throughout childhood and into adulthood. Early damage can be reversed. We can positively affect the way abused or neglected children view themselves, but this involves changing their unconscious memories and beliefs.

Unconscious memory is non-verbal and probably develops pre-birth. It is present at birth, and continues throughout life. The unconscious memory stores the 'blueprints', or 'inner mental models' that are formed in the early months of life. The brain recognizes repeated experiences, sees the patterns and then predicts an outcome. This is the 'blueprint'. For example, a hungry baby signals to the primary carer by crying. The carer recognizes the baby's distress, in this case hunger, and responds appropriately. Baby is again comfortable and calm. The baby learns that his/her cry will bring food from the carer, and the carer is able to 'read' the child and to understand and meet the need. This understanding is attunement, the foundation of a healthy attachment.

The implications of laying down positive unconscious mental models are immense. It is through this process that the baby's sense of self-worth and trust in adults is formed. If the adult understands their baby's signals and responds appropriately, the baby feels valued and nurtured. This is the start of developing positive self-esteem. At the same time, the baby also experiences the world (at this stage provided by the primary carer) as a safe place. The baby feels that the adult can be trusted to ensure that he/she is comfortable. We have attunement and trust – the essence of a secure attachment.

Poor, neglectful or inconsistent parenting has the opposite effect. If a baby cries and no one responds, stress levels increase. He/she cries louder and, if still ignored, begins to scream. The accompanying physical changes indicate a sharp rise in stress hormones, an increased heart rate, red face and sweating. With no response, the baby will eventually fall asleep – still hungry and uncomfortable, but exhausted. If this is a regular pattern, babies' inner mental models tell them they are not understood, not heard and not important. There is no attunement. Low self-worth and a mistrust of adults are already developing – the essence of an insecure attachment.

A child removed from neglectful or abusive parents before the first or second birthday may have no conscious memories, but the negative models will already be imprinted in the unconscious memory. If a young child is particularly placid, never cries and is very compliant, it could mean that he/she had just given up hope of being noticed. Their inner mental model is telling him/her that there is just no point in making a fuss! If not addressed, these unconscious beliefs will continue to adversely affect the child's behaviour and development.

At any age, a particularly frightening experience will cause stress levels to rise dramatically. The increased hormones released in the brain actually block the way memories are processed and stored. Traumatic memories are thus redirected and stored in the unconscious part of the brain. Such memories are literally blocked out and may only 'leak' into the conscious memory, perhaps at a much later stage via night terrors or flashbacks. Children may have no conscious memories of early terrifying experiences, but they carry the trauma with them, in their bodies. At some stage their behaviour will reflect this.

Older children who have experienced early trauma may have developed sophisticated language skills, but their mental models are still in the unconscious/preverbal stage, and emotionally they may remain immature. Positive language is not enough to overlay those negative models. Telling children that neglect or abuse was not their fault will have limited impact. They need to believe this, from the inside.

The negative blueprints will always be there but, as the brain is malleable and constantly developing, it is possible to tap back into the unconscious and overlay those damaging mental models with affirming ones. By reading their signals accurately, interpreting their behaviour and responding appropriately, children can be helped to develop a more positive sense of themselves, adults and the world.

Children in care often remain confused about their early history and blame themselves for their neglect. They may feel a deep sense of shame. They do not have the inner resources to unravel past events or to process feelings about this on their own. Some will find it too painful and will avoid discussing such issues directly. If left unaddressed, these feelings will fester and may lead to further worrying or challenging behaviour in the future.

We have to understand the children we are responsible for. To achieve this we must keep these theories and their interconnections in mind. Life work techniques that gently engage the unconscious mind can, over time, be very successful in helping children to overlay some of their negative inner beliefs.

Continued research in neuroscience may unlock more secrets of the brain. In future, this may help further in our search for the most appropriate life work techniques and interventions, ones that can access the unconscious, stimulate new neural pathways, repair the damage and overlay the child's negative internal working model with a more positive one.

CHAPTER 4

The Team Around the Child

The local authority has a duty to ensure that life work is undertaken with all children in care. Delays in starting or in completing certain aspects of this work often occur because of misunderstandings and differences of opinion about who should actually be undertaking this work, when and which worker or agency is responsible.

There is a team around the child. Between them, the members of this team should have a comprehensive overview. They are in the best position to ensure that – regardless of the age of the child or his/her circumstances – a life work plan is in place. Some elements of life work begin as soon as the child comes into care. Indeed, in some instances, it begins prior to the child being looked after, and it should continue throughout his/her journey in care and into adulthood.

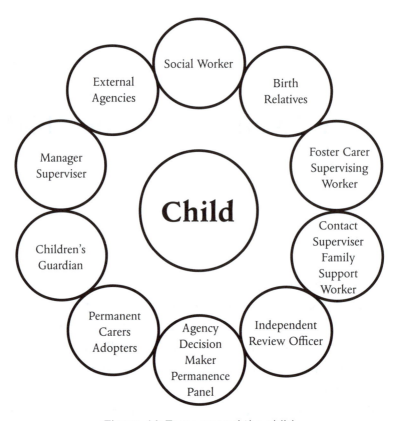

Figure 4.1: Team around the child

The child's social worker

In most social care agencies, it is the child's social worker, often referred to as the 'key worker', who is responsible for ensuring that life work is completed. The social worker, in consultation with their supervisor, holds key responsibility for drawing up the care plan, including the life work plan. This plan is discussed and agreed at the looked after children's statutory review, although some agencies have separate life work planning meetings.

The social worker is responsible for coordinating the agreed life work, and ensuring that the appropriate aspect of the work is in place. He/she must record the plan and update it in the child's records, preferably in a section specifically dedicated to life work.

Adoption guidance also suggests that the 'life story book and memory box should be coordinated by one person, preferably the child's social worker' (*Adoption: Statutory Guidance* 2013, Adoption Agency Regulation 35). Similarly, the guidance implies that the child's social worker should compile the later life letter.

Social workers are clearly responsible for many aspects of life work. It is a fundamental part of their role, but social workers should not necessarily be expected to actually *do* all of this work. They are not working in isolation. Indeed, the 'expectation that one person is proficient in all areas associated with life work is unrealistic and naïve' (Nicholls 2005, p.14). If the child is placed for adoption, for instance, the social worker may have undertaken some direct work with the child, prior to the move, the foster carer should take some responsibility for the memory box, while a colleague in the adoption team may be in the best position to compile the life story book. Cooperation and negotiation are needed to ensure the best outcome for the child.

In many instances, a carer or worker from another team or agency may be identified as the most appropriate person to undertake some aspects of this work. Indeed, Ryan and Walker (2016) suggest that 'any sympathetic adult who is prepared to spend time and give the commitment to the child…can be the right person' (p 10).

While care proceedings are in progress the social worker's focus is on gathering evidence and preparing statements for the court. There are strict timescales and pressure to give this priority. Most care proceedings are contested and the birth family may, understandably, feel upset and angry. It is not unusual for social workers to be threatened and to experience verbal and, in some instances, physical abuse from members of the birth family around this time. It may be impossible and insensitive to expect the social worker to involve the birth parents in life work at this stage. However, others involved, perhaps the foster carer or contact supervisor, may be able to start this, in an indirect and less threatening way.

As with all service users, children must be treated with respect and their diversity valued. In all interactions, including life work, the social worker must consider the child's specific and additional needs: gender, sexual orientation, ethnic origin, culture, religious beliefs, learning difficulties, mental and physical health issues and disabilities. Children are unique and some will have very complex care needs. Communication methods and techniques must be tailored to the child's specific needs.

With so many expectations and tasks to complete, it would be unusual for one worker to have the depth of knowledge to feel confident in all areas. Seeking advice and information and, in some instances, co-working with colleagues who have skills or expertise in particular fields is essential. This could be internally, from another specialist team, or externally involving schools, the health service or specific agencies and charities. This inclusive approach will ensure that children receive the best possible service.

Birth relatives

For children who remain in substitute care, the birth families' contributions are vital. The birth family still has significant legal rights in relation to their children. Their views must be taken into account throughout the time the child is in care. They are the most significant source of information about the child's early experiences and the family's history. They can provide details of ethnic origin, culture and religious beliefs, as well as the more personal details so important to children.

As noted, birth parents may not feel able to consider life work during care proceedings. They may feel too distressed or too angry to cooperate, and reluctant to share information or photographs.

Many are able to contribute at a later stage, or other members of the birth family – grandparents, aunties or uncles – may be able to help.

Being more creative in the way we approach birth parents in relation to life work may also be productive. Many have experienced difficult and traumatic childhoods themselves. Some have drug or alcohol dependency, mental health problems or learning difficulties. Expressing themselves verbally or in writing may not come easily. They may welcome the opportunity of sharing information using a different medium.

Life work tools and colourful activity sheets used with children may prove less threatening, more enjoyable and a more effective method of gathering details. Some birth parents may be able to share their thoughts and to give some factual as well as 'soft' information about themselves in this less direct and playful way. Birth family members' favourite foods, films, songs or television programmes, shoe sizes, hand- or footprints, happy or funny memories, drawings and anecdotes about themselves and the child could be gathered. Such details are not easily found on the child's looked after records.

Birth parents must also be given the opportunity to express their views and their understanding of the events leading to their child becoming looked after. This may be very different from the views of the professionals, but their perception should be recorded.

If possible, birth relatives should be encouraged to contribute directly to the life work with the child. In some circumstances, involving members of the family could help with disengagement work. It could help to dispel some of the child's fantasies, and in some instances it might give them 'permission' to move on and attach to their new family.

If adoption or permanency is the plan, birth relatives should be encouraged to write a letter or record a message that could be shared with the child at a later stage.

Foster carer and supervising social worker

Foster carers are a very influential part of the team around the child. They must 'encourage the child to reflect on and understand his/her history, according to the child's age and ability, and to keep appropriate memorabilia'. They must 'record significant life events for the child, and encourage the child to make such recordings, including photograph albums' (*Fostering Services: National Minimum Standards* 2011). This applies to local authority and independent fostering agencies.

Using memory boxes and compiling memory books can help children make sense of life events and may be the best way of preserving important memories. This process should begin as soon as the child is fostered and continue throughout the time the child lives with the foster carer.

The child's foster carer is also in a position to do much of the informal life work, as they have responsibility for day-to-day care. Children are more likely to spontaneously ask questions and seek explanations from them about why they are in care or what the future holds.

It is concerning to hear that some foster carers have limited knowledge of the children's previous experiences, although they may have been caring for them for weeks or even months. To answer the children's questions sensitively, they must have a good understanding of the child's history. They will also need to process the details, and must be supported in thinking through explanations and honest responses.

Direct work can also be more productive when the main carer is involved. However, for this to be successful they need to understand the benefits and significance of the games and techniques used. The foster carers must be able to contain their own emotions and feelings. They need to provide nurture, acceptance and a sense of safety during the life work sessions. Their ability to fulfill this role will need to be assessed before they are involved. If they are not 'on board' they may inadvertently sabotage the sessions. Preparation needs to be done with them and their supervising officer first. Further training in this area may be needed.

Foster carers also play a vital role in preparing children for transitions. 'To the child, the temporary primary carers are a link to their past and the bridge to their future' (Nicholls 2005, p.30). They will be involved, not only in preparing the child for the move, but also in preparing the adults, whether that is the birth family, another foster placement or adopters.

Although many details will be passed on verbally, a simple but comprehensive booklet of essential information about the child, their routines and everyday care, should always be completed by the foster carer. This booklet will be a helpful reference for the next placement. It captures a snapshot of the child's life at that time. It is another very useful aid to any future life work. The new carer should keep this safe and, if the child moves again, it goes with them. A copy should also be retained on the child's file (Appendix A).

The foster carer may have looked after the child for many months, or even years. As the primary attachment figure they must use their skills to prepare the child for the transition, but they also need support to acknowledge their own feelings about this move. They may be very pleased for the child, or possibly relieved. There may also be sadness and a sense of loss, and this will have an impact on their family life.

The fostering supervising social worker assesses and reviews carers, and has primary responsibility for advice and support. They know the carer's strengths and limitations and can provide appropriate training to enhance their skills. They should ensure that foster carers understand the purpose of life work, appreciate their pivotal role, and have the appropriate tools and equipment to enable them to fulfill their responsibilities. If using foster carers from other local authorities, or from private agencies, expectations in relation to their role in life work should be clear. Their policies and guidance in relation to this should also be available.

Contact supervisors and family support workers

Most children have regular and frequent contact with birth family members during the early weeks and months of being in care. Maintaining family relationships is important and a contact or family support worker usually supervises these sessions. If the child is to return home, they can help to prepare and advise the birth parents on a very practical level, particularly in relation to babies and very young children.

The contact supervisor often establishes a more relaxed rapport with the birth family than the social worker. In the event of a child remaining in care, he/she may be able to engage both the child and the birth parents in some 'all about me' activity sheets. They could do some simple play-related activities, such as drawing each other or making hand- or footprints. The child may wish to keep such mementos in their memory box or book. Birth parents may be happy for contact supervisors to take photographs during these sessions, and copies can be made available for them, the child and the social worker.

Independent reviewing officer

While the child is in care, the local authority must hold regular looked after children reviews, to consider the care plan and to ensure that the best possible outcomes are achieved. These meetings provide an opportunity for the team around the child to work together on all aspects of the care plan, including the life work plan.

The child's social worker, members of the birth family, foster carers, family support workers, contact supervisors, nursery or school staff may attend the review. Depending on age, understanding and if willing, the child may also attend all or part of the meeting.

Reviews are chaired by Independent Reviewing Officers (IRO's). They have a crucial role in ensuring that the local authority fulfils its responsibilities, as corporate parents, for all children in care.

There was concern that some IRO's were not sufficiently robust in challenging decisions made, even if they felt plans were not in the child's best interest. Reviews were in danger of becoming a 'sterile box ticking exercise' (Care Matters Green Paper Consultation 2006–7). The Children and Young Persons Act 2008 introduced some key changes and the IRO's role has been strengthened. They now review and monitor the plans. They must have 'an effective independent oversight of the child's case and ensure that the child's interests are protected throughout the care panning process' and 'where necessary, challenge poor practice' (IRO Handbook 2010).

As part of the care plan, the life work plan should be addressed at the first statutory review (a month after the child comes into care), and again at the second review, (4 months after the child comes into care). This is when all permanence options, including reunification, are considered. Following this, reviews are held every six months. Appropriate life work and different roles and responsibilities should be addressed at all reviews. Timescales and progress should be recorded and the IRO also holds some responsibility for quality assuring this work.

IRO's have a duty to promote 'the voice of child'. They must speak with children before reviews and listen to their views. They should discuss the care plan and help them to understand why certain decisions have been or are being made. This is direct life work.

One of the qualifications required of an IRO is 'the ability to communicate with children and young people'. In relation to very young children it is acknowledged that 'Observing the child or interacting with him/her, for example in play or by reading ... may be a more appropriate way of establishing the child's feelings and understanding' (IRO Guideline 2010 3.35).

Knowledge of life work techniques is therefore implicit in the role of the IRO. While they must ensure that some aspects of life work are done, they also have a responsibility to contribute directly to this work.

Agency Decision Maker and Adoption and Permanency Panel

When permanent fostering or adoption is the care plan, the Adoption and Permanence Panel recommends, and the Agency Decision Maker (ADM) agrees or disagrees with this plan. Details of life work already completed and future work planned should be included in the comprehensive Child's Permanence Report (CPR), that is prepared for the ADM and panel.

If the panel is considering the match of a child with prospective adopters or permanent carers, they will seek confirmation that some aspect of life work has started. If the plan is adoption, this will include the life story book and later life letter.

The panel has an independent quality assurance role in relation to the work of the agency, including life work. Some panels insist on seeing drafts of the book and letter, before agreeing the match. The adopters or permanent carers should be involved in the final versions, so these are more effectively completed after the Adoption Order has been granted, and after the Celebratory Hearing.

Permanent carer and adopter

Children in permanent foster placements, and those who are adopted, should have had some preparation prior to their move. They may have some of the more tangible components of life work (e.g. a life work folder, a memory book and box and a photograph album). Children living with permanent substitute families should also have a life story book and, if adopted, a later life letter. These essential tools remind the adults about the child's early experiences, and help them to understand the history from the child's perspective. They make a significant contribution to the process of attunement and attachment.

There is an expectation that long-term carers and adopters will continue life work with their children. Much of this will be done spontaneously and informally. Sadly, many children, despite having spent the majority of their childhoods in care, will not have any of these tools. This is a great disservice to the children and to their families. It means that carers and adopters have not been provided with the foundation that can empower and enable them to continue effective and attuned life work with their children. It is never too late to put this right.

Children in long-term fostering placements remain in care. Their carers continue to receive support from the child's social worker and from their fostering supervising worker, so the lack of life work tools can easily be addressed. Local authorities also provide Adoption Support Services. An adoption worker may remain in contact and continue to advise adopters for months or, in some instances, years after the child is adopted. Post-placement workshops and training on aspects of life work are available for carers and adopters, if not locally then through other national organizations like Adoption UK or the Fostering Network. There are plenty of opportunities for carers and adopters to increase their knowledge and skills in this area.

Children's Guardian

When care proceedings are initiated, the Children and Families Court Advisory and Support Service (Cafcass) will allocate a

Children's Guardian. Guardians are not employed by the court or by the local authority. They are completely independent.

Guardians scrutinize the local authority's care plan and make recommendations to the court. They view records, speak to practitioners, attend planning meetings and observe contact sessions. They also see members of the birth family and other significant people in the child's life.

In a relatively short time, they must get to know the children they represent, because in court they are 'the voice of the child'. Depending on the child's level of understanding, they discuss the local authority's concerns and proposed care plans and assess his/her thoughts and feelings. They need to use appropriate methods of communication. For this, Guardians employ many of the life work techniques used by other practitioners.

When courts make a final decision, Guardians (along with the foster carer and social worker) spend time using life journey tools to help the child to begin to understand why this decision was made and to explain the future plans.

Manager and supervisor

Working with children and with birth families raises many dilemmas and conflicting emotions for the professionals involved, especially those responsible for drawing up and implementing care plans and initiating care proceedings. Some observations and much of the information and evidence gathered is distressing. Presenting this in court can be an intimidating and emotionally draining experience.

Social workers often need time to recover and reflect on this ordeal, before they can begin to help the child to understand the decisions that have been made. In most agencies, once care proceedings have been completed, a different team and worker are introduced. They will also need time to prepare, reflect and process the child's information before they can do any direct work. Ideally several joint handover sessions with the child and carer should be planned.

In some instances it may be more appropriate for any direct life journey work to be allocated to someone other than the key worker. Whoever undertakes it must have the space to plan and to commit to it. The timescales must be realistic and agreed with supervisors. 'Direct work can be both time-consuming and professionally challenging…the worker needs to be functioning in a professional and supportive climate where adequate time is available to plan, record and evaluate sessions' (Triseliotis 1999, p.115).

Regular, reflective supervision with managers who understand the nature and appreciate the different aspects of life work is imperative. Clear guidelines and suggestions are essential. Group supervision or consultation sessions, across teams, can provide excellent opportunities for colleagues to learn from each other, as they share experiences, ideas and resources.

Managers should encourage and nurture the expertise in their workforce, so that those with more experience of life work, can mentor others and offer support.

External agencies

Access to consultants from a range of disciplines may prove invaluable when considering the best approach. The duty of 'corporate parenting' covers all members of the local council, and any services provided by them. Some aspects of life work may be appropriately commissioned to outside agencies.

Some children have complex needs and need more intense therapeutic life work. Independent specialists, therapists and private agencies are able to offer a more concentrated service, although such resources are relatively scarce and, for many local authorities, the cost is prohibitive. Currently, the government's Adoption Support Fund makes these services more available for some adopted children and for those living with Special Guardians. However, this fund only covers a minority of children needing life work, and it may not be a permanent provision.

Local authorities have a duty of care and 'a legal responsibility to ensure that the needs of children and young people in their care are prioritized' (SCIE/NICE 2010, p.2). Effective life work is central in meeting these needs; social care providers must invest in this area of work.

The cost for the children of not doing so is high: As Buchanan's research (2014) involving care leavers confirmed: 'Many of the young people were able to reflect on the consequences they had experienced as a result of an incoherent narrative and missing information, with some reporting issues with mental health, self-esteem, physical ill health and difficulties with relationships' (Buchanan 2014, p.123).

CHAPTER 5

Aspects of Life Work

Life work has many layers and different aspects. It should start gently, in a non-direct way and progress at a pace that is comfortable, not only for the child, but also for the workers involved. If adults seem uneasy or embarrassed, the child will pick up on this discomfort rather than their words. It's not only what we say. It's the way that we say it. Children notice tone of voice and body language.

Life work is an integral part of the social work task. It is a constant and on going process and, if done appropriately and with sensitivity, it can have lifelong benefits. The child is always the focus, but is not always directly involved in all aspects of this work.

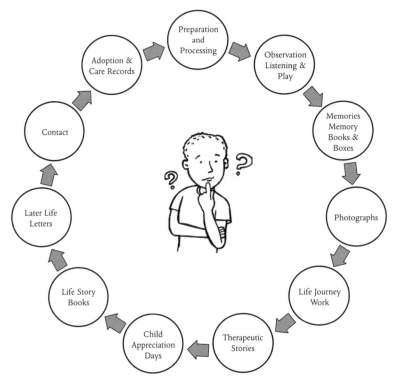

Figure 5.1: Aspects of Life Work

Preparation and processing

The first stage of life work should begin as soon as the child comes into care and, indeed, if the child is relinquished or if the placement is planned, then this should start before the child is looked after.

Previous interventions designed to prevent the child coming into care, such as 'Signs of Safety', may have been used. This approach involves children directly and aims to give them an understanding of what has happened, and why child protection services are involved in their care.

Signs of Safety is a solution focused approach and 'aims to work collaboratively and in partnership with families and children to conduct risk assessments' (Bunn 2013, p.7). Child-friendly worksheets are used to explore the child's anxieties and concerns, e.g. The Three Houses (Bunn 2013, p.30).

Starting with the 'House of Good Things', the child is encouraged to think about the positive and enjoyable things in their lives, before moving on to the 'House of Worries'. Here, things not liked about life at home are considered. Finally, the child moves to the 'House of Dreams', where thoughts and ideas about the ideal home life are explored. What would need to change and what would happen there? Who would be with the child? The concept of a house can be adapted and could be a flat, a caravan, a room, etc. If the child comes into care, this work could provide a springboard for further life work. The direct work tools used by this, and other child protection and early preventative programmes, should be familiar and available to all children's teams.

This is a time to gather as much information as possible about the child in the present, as well as his/her previous experiences and family history. There could be contributions from birth parents, extended family members, friends or other significant adults. Other agencies involved – including schools, nurseries and health professionals – may also hold essential information. The child too is, of course, a primary source of information. Babies and non-verbal children are still able to 'tell' us so much about themselves and their experiences. They can make their 'voices' heard, indirectly, but loudly, through their presentation and behaviour.

During the early weeks or months of placement, there is usually frequent contact between the child, members of the birth family and the social worker. For some children the plan may be reunification, for others the future is more uncertain, but life work must continue.

This preparation stage is essential, irrespective of the care plan, child's age and cognitive ability or their willingness to participate. It does not necessarily involve the child directly. This is the time for the adults concerned in the child's care to begin to process the history themselves. As Nicholls notes, 'a significant part of the preparatory work is done *for* the child as opposed to *with* the child…whether or not the child is willing or able to take part at that time' (Nicholls 2005, p.21)

For those embarking on life work at a later stage in the child's journey in care, gathering and processing information about the child's early experiences and family is still the first step. Taking time to read previous reports is essential.

Most agencies now use electronic files, so contemporaneous notes, scribbled observations or anecdotes may no longer be available. This can make it harder to gain a true sense of the child's experiences. 'The chatty, detailed style of recording of previous decades was abandoned in favour of a more business-like approach, in which it was often hard to find in the file the real child… Children's stories were lost' (Baynes 2008, p.44). Nevertheless, an electronic file search still provides vital information. Talking to previous social workers and foster carers, if available, and to members of the birth family, or to anyone who has knowledge of the child, may fill some gaps.

All children in care have experienced separation and loss. Some have suffered extreme neglect and abuse. Their stories are likely to evoke strong emotions in the adults involved. They need time to process the information and 'take a step back' before they try to help the child to process it.

It is important that adults do not pre-empt or stifle the child's feelings and responses, or overwhelm them with their own emotional reactions. As Rose warns, 'As we work with children who grieve, remember our own wounds can be reopened. Children need us to separate our losses from theirs, so that they can stay connected to their own experience without feeling the need to protect us from being hurt' (Rose 2012, n.p.)

Observation, listening and play

Adults should tread carefully, taking time to get to know and to tune into the child before embarking on any direct work. Observing children at play, and listening to their interactions with other children, with adults and with their toys is the best way of exploring their inner world. Their play tells us so much about their thoughts and feelings, how they see themselves, how they view adults and what they make of the world in general.

This stage of life work involves engagement, building rapport and trust. It's a time to gently glean information about the child: their interests, likes and dislikes; their hopes and their fears. Life work is not about 'jumping in' and talking *at* children. First, we must listen and gain a sense of what the child knows or thinks he/she knows about their early experiences and why they are not able to live with their birth families.

Life work may later involve verifying and validating the child memories or it may entail helping them to consider other explanations. At this stage, listening to the child and their primary carer is more important than trying to address any misconceptions directly.

Memories, memory books and boxes

Memories – both happy and sad – shape who we are and help us to understand ourselves and those around us. Children brought up in their birth families are frequently told stories about themselves and their extended family and, without realizing, they become immersed in their history. Family gatherings, celebrations, festivals or funerals, all provide opportunities to remember, to exchange childhood and family anecdotes, and to laugh or to cry.

The stories we are told, and other people's memories of us, play an important part in giving us a sense of self. Our identity evolves naturally over time. 'Identity is something that we gather and form along life's path…it is a myriad of interconnecting fragments of memory and experience… Anecdotal stories surrounding culture, family and life events that often preceded one's own existence' (Nicholls 2005, p.6). For children separated from their birth families, especially those who experience multiple placements, these stories and memories are so easily lost.

As already noted, most case records are now collated and stored electronically. Hard facts and dates are logged. The emphasis is on clear analysis. Veering into subjective descriptions, feelings and opinions has long been discouraged. Assessments, court statements and other social work reports tend to focus on the difficulties, and on providing evidence. They capture sad, painful and unhappy experiences. They highlight birth parents' limitations or difficulties and assess the detrimental impact on the child's wellbeing. The 'soft' descriptive information – the stories and any positive experiences – may be overlooked, not recorded and forever lost to the child.

Memory books and memory boxes are an attempt to redress the balance by recording and preserving some of the child's more positive experiences. Once in care, the foster carer has prime responsibility for collating and recording these. It is a statutory requirement and the fostering supervising officer should be guiding and supporting the foster carer with this task.

Every child is unique, so each memory book or box can be customized and the content will be different. The box could contain some welcoming items to help the foster carer and child begin this task. Other memorabilia can be added over time, remembering that names, dates, lists of contents or labels are important, so that the significance of each item is not lost.

Foster carers can capture happy childhood experiences in words, photographs, videos, certificates and other memorabilia.

Birth relatives, family friends, social workers, contact supervisors, nursery staff and teachers could all contribute to the book by adding their stories and positive or funny memories of the child.

Memories are of course also sensory. A perfume, aftershave or smell of washing powder on a child's blanket or cuddly toy may trigger strong feelings. Similarly, the sound of a voice on a video or recorded music, or the feel of a particular object in the memory box may be extremely evocative. These could be happy, sad or fearful memories.

Memory books and memory boxes belong to the children. If they return home, move to another foster home, or on to adoptive parents, these will go with them. For children who remain in care, the adults have a duty to ensure that the book and the box are kept safe and secure. The contents can help the child to incorporate the past more comfortably into the present. Capturing happy memories provides balance and can help to shape a more positive future.

Photographs

Photographs are another key element of life work and every effort should be made to obtain images of birth parents, siblings, other birth relatives, foster carers, adopters, friends and any significant people in the child's life. Names (first names only are advisable, with reference to data protection and identifying information), relationships and dates should be added. Although copies of some of the photographs should be placed or scanned into the child's memory book and life story book, all looked after children should also have a separate and clearly labelled photograph album.

Taking photographs has never been easier. Many of us now have hundreds of digital images on mobile phones, tablets or computers. Despite this, for children moving through the care system, there is a danger that these digital prints will not be preserved. They may not be stored electronically in a secure but accessible folder, or not passed on with the child to the next placement. Many photographs are lost 'somewhere' in transition or on the IT system.

Hard copies of a selection of photographs are invaluable and again this is something that foster carers should collate from the time the child is placed with them. A sturdy, traditional photograph album provides something tangible that the child and carer/adopters can enjoy and share. It should contain not only photographs of the child and important people in their lives, but also photographs of the home, the child's bedroom, garden or local park, nursery or school. Perhaps a photograph of a local shop where the child bought sweets on a Saturday, or the bakers where he/she could choose a cake on the way home from school.

Special occasions, but also everyday ordinary events, should be captured to provide a pictorial record of the child's journey. Add captions, dates, names and relationship to the child, but be wary of including identifying third party information.

Foster carers often have framed photographs of their own children, nephews, nieces or grandchildren proudly displayed on their shelves and mantelpieces. The message is clear: these children are loved, claimed and belong to this family. Children in care also deserve to feel that they too are loveable, valued and welcomed as part of the family, even if the placement is a relatively short term one. So, unless there is a cultural or religious objection to displaying photographs, all children in care or adopted should also have framed images of themselves, at various ages. They are all worthy of being proudly displayed.

Life journey work

This aspect of life work always involves the child and, as noted previously, it is also referred to as direct work or life story work. It can be further divided into informal or formal.

Much informal life journey work just happens spontaneously. During the social worker's regular statutory visits, at contact sessions, on walks home from school or over lunch with the foster carer or adopter, the child may ask: 'Why didn't my birth mother turn up for contact?' 'Why couldn't she look after me?' 'Why can't I see my birth father?' 'When can I go home?' Many of these questions can be answered sensitively, and honestly, as they arise. If you are unsure of the explanation or need time to reflect on the wording before responding, simply say so. Acknowledge that the question is an 'important' or 'interesting' one, and do not forget to get back to them. There may be no definitive answers, but just acknowledging their questions and encouraging reflective dialogue can be extremely fruitful. Saying 'I wonder if …' gives room for considering options and thinking aloud discussions.

Children often ask the most searching questions, or share their worries and concerns, at times when they don't have to make eye contact, for example while the adult is driving. Indeed, car journeys can be a productive time in this regard, and some use this and organize their cars as a play space. 'Children often find the rhythm soothing and not being able to make eye contact a positive advantage, increasing their ability to feel safe' (Tait and Wosu 2013, p.24).

When to begin more formal life journey work sessions with the child can prove more contentious, particularly if the child isn't asking any questions directly. The age-old conundrum: 'What comes first, the chicken or the egg?' springs to mind. The child may never be ready, until some life work has been done.

Many practitioners believe that this work should not start until the child has a secure base, i.e. until settled in a permanent placement. If this approach is adopted, many children in care could spend months, or even years, living 'in limbo', with confusion and misconceptions. Many care leavers enter adulthood still not understanding why they have spent so many years in care.

Some are depressed or full of rage or self-loathing, as their feelings of being unlovable and of shame and self-blame can become overwhelming. For some, that stable placement remains elusive.

Others believe this work is not appropriate during the early weeks of placement, particularly while various assessments are being completed and, if care proceedings are in progress, they do not want to pre-empt the court's decision. For the child, this silent period could allow fears and fantasies to develop and it is fertile ground for those seeds of 'badness' and self-blame to flourish.

Children need honest and clear explanations about why they are in care and what the concerns are, as soon as possible. For some children, using simple activity sheets (e.g. Appendix B 'Why did I come into care?') allows the worker and child to explore different perspectives. It acknowledges that there are several explanations and that the social worker's and the birth family's viewpoints may be contradictory. The judge will listen to all these views, including the child's, and make the very important decisions about the future. This simple and truthful explanation is what children need and deserve.

If reunification is agreed, the child will need to know what has changed. In some circumstances he/she will seek reassurance about why it is now safe to return home. We can never assume that this is something that all children will welcome. If a Care Order is granted, the child should know why the judge felt that he/she should remain in care. The Children's Guardian has a major role to play in this, and explanations should involve the foster carer and social worker too. The child may be upset or relieved. As many practitioners know, having confirmation that they will not be going home is a time when some children feel safe enough to make further disclosures of abuse.

Whatever the decision of the court, there is work to be done with the child and the birth family, to prepare for the return home or for future care options.

Baynes believes that 'children need to be involved in the decision to start life story work, but all too often they are required rather than invited to participate'. She is concerned that the work should start at a time right for the child rather than an 'organisational requirement' (Baynes 2008, p.47). The timing must be right for the child, but we must not forget that life work is indeed a statutory requirement.

The Children Act 1989, and all subsequent related legislation, emphasizes the importance of ensuring that the child's views and wishes are ascertained. The 'voice' of the child must be heard. Hearing that voice requires life work as children's thoughts and feelings are often reflected more accurately in their play, rather than in their words. As Baynes also points out, 'the interactive nature of play helps to ensure that the work is done with (rather than to) the child' (Baynes 2008, p.47).

Furthermore, we need to be mindful of miscommunication and the 'wall of silence' that can build up between child and adult. Children are often afraid to ask questions, fear the answers, or are just not sure what to ask. Sydney and Price (2014) advise using 'natural triggers' to invite conversations and note that, 'Children do not often have the words to ask the questions that can help them to make sense of their experiences, nor indeed be aware of the questions they may have' (Sydney and Price 2014, p.114). Many loving and well-meaning adoptive parents mistakenly believe that their children are disinterested in their histories. The child doesn't ask, so they don't raise the topic. They fear doing so will upset the child or 'rock the boat'.

Conversely, many adult adoptees comment that, while always knowing they were adopted, they knew little about the circumstances leading to this. From a young age they picked up on the body language, tension or tone of voice of their adoptive parents. They sensed that this was a topic that made the adults feel uncomfortable. They assumed they were the cause of this discomfort. Some stopped asking questions, for fear of upsetting their adoptive parents.

Some of the older adopted adults I counselled lived, for many years, with a sense of shame and dread before 'summoning up the courage' to seek access to their records. They came to find the missing pieces of their 'jigsaws'. Invariably, the fears about their history were unfounded. The burden of carrying that heavy 'not knowing' was lifted, and was noticably reflected in their whole, much lighter, demeanour.

Recently, a teenager commented that, from a young age, he had been aware of his adoptive mother's reluctance to talk about his birth family. He noted that whenever a television programme involved adoption, she looked 'very uncomfortable'. She would invariably make an excuse to leave the room, thus avoiding discussion. He was desperate to know more about his early history, but was reluctant to approach his adoptive mother. The silence continued.

For foster carers, and practitioners too, there is a danger that opportunities to initiate conversation with children are missed for fear of upsetting or destabilizing the placement. Talking to children about 'adult matters creates a form of panic resulting in some practitioners and carers taking flight, and resorting to the denial of need' (Nicholls 2005, p.8).

Some workers feel that they don't have the skills to do this work. They express anxiety about how to start and worry that they will 'get it all wrong', or fear that they could do more harm than good and may re-traumatize the child. They are not sure what to do or how to engage children in this task. 'Sometimes children suffer longer than they should…because the adults around them lack the skills to open the door to effective communication' (Tait and Wosu 2013, p.9). However, the ability to be playful is the main requirement.

It was practitioners' anxiety that inspired Wrench and Naylor to put many of their tried and tested practical activities into a book to show them 'just how to *do* it' (Wrench and Naylor 2013, p.9). They have both worked within local authorities and are well aware of the current pressures. Their book contains numerous ideas and examples of life work techniques. Simple explanations and guidance are provided, along with resources needed for each activity. Tait and Wosu (2013) also provide inspiration and suggest many ways of starting this work with 'playful activities and strategies to open communication with vulnerable children'.

Rose (2012) advocates a life story therapy approach. He is an expert in this field and, like other independent specialists, he is able to commit to consistent, regular sessions. He provides predictability and reliability, and is usually involved in working directly with the child for a period of 18 months or longer.

Inspiration and ideas can be taken from Rose's approach, but local authority children's practitioners can seldom commit to this level of intensity. Many are working with several chaotic, disorganized children and families, and dealing with volatile situations on a daily basis. Sudden placement disruptions, exclusions from school, missing children, revised court dates, etc. mean that some rescheduling of appointments and re-prioritizing of tasks is unavoidable. It is difficult to replicate the consistency, but the local authority's input is imperative. Practitioners can be mindful, fully present and available when with the child. Distractions can be avoided (e.g. mobile phones switched off).

Rose (2012) uses easy, fun ways to engage children: a game of 'join the dots' or Jenga, (Timber) involving him, the child and the primary carer, as ice-breakers. His use of life journey mapping or wallpaper work is particularly effective. This is a graphic way of helping children to explore and understand past events. Rolls of wallpaper are used to explore the child's history. He includes details of birth family, their lives and experiences prior to the birth of the child, and plots the child's life up to the present time. He uses this information for the basis of the life story book. When the wallpaper work is completed, he encourages the child and carer to literally walk along and experience the child's life journey together.

This and many of his other techniques can be adapted and used with children of all ages. Wallpaper work may involve drawing, painting, writing, using clipart, cutting and sticking. Some children use their artistic talents to recreate their journey. Most become engrossed in the activity and it usually takes many sessions to complete. It involves sitting on the floor, looking down (so no direct eye contact needed) and concentrating on the task in hand, perhaps colouring in, cutting out or sticking: activities that can provide opportunities for accessing those unconscious beliefs and thoughts.

The end product can look very 'messy' – often a very accurate reflection of child's life. But, it is this very 'mess' that may enable the child to gain a much clearer understanding of their life journey. Their life map can become 'organized chaos'. When completed, children know what's there and where to find it. It makes sense to them.

Other books packed with practical tips and enjoyable, effective life journey work activities are included in the suggested reading list.

Involve the main attachment figure in the life work sessions if he/she is able to support and interact positively with the child. Being part of the activities increases understanding and empathy, as they hear directly from the child their recollections and misconceptions. It will help them tune into the child, to consider more appropriate re-parenting techniques, and will have a beneficial impact on their relationship.

Before beginning direct work, use your knowledge of the child to think about the timing of sessions and appropriate activities. How much can the child manage? Think about their interests, level of cognitive development and functioning rather than age. Choose a few of the simple techniques that you are comfortable with, and that feel right for the child, and 'just do it'. Be flexible and if one activity doesn't feel right, try another one. Go at the child's pace and have fun.

Life journey work can be placed in a folder or into the child's memory box and kept for or by the child. Scans, photocopies or photographs of the work should also be retained on the child's records. Some may appreciate electronic copies of the work when completed. However it is preserved, it should always be available to revisit and build on as the child matures.

Many children, and some professionals, find using digital technology a more comfortable and more effective way of working. This approach is becoming popular when working with teenagers although, as with all life work techniques, there is no age limit. Some of the simple, playful traditional approaches will work with older children. Some of the digital techniques will appeal to young ones.

Certainly, for most adolescents, smartphones and social media tend to be the favoured methods of staying in touch with friends, family and with the wider world. Using familiar technologies and preferred modes of communication may be a helpful starting place for life work. 'Digital life work projects seek to empower young people to make use of the everyday accessible digital technologies that many appear to be glued to' (Hammond in Ryan and Walker 2016, p.111).

Hammond has written extensively about the effectiveness of digital life story work with young people in care. He acknowledges that it is not a 'magic wand' or 'immediate solution'. Teenagers do not suddenly become 'reflective', but these techniques can be a 'very appealing and powerful' way of engaging them.

Digital life work can involve: tablets, laptops, computers, cameras, videos or audio recorders, through creating 'soundscapes', 'photo mash ups', 'digital comic strips', 'pod walks' and 'virtual walks'. Hammond and Cooper (2013) supports and encourages the young person to reflect on their life and process their experiences. As with traditional life journey work, there will be a finished 'product' and instead of a book it could be a photo collage, soundtrack or short film.

Therapeutic stories

Stories and storytelling lie at the heart of human experience. Through stories we share events, beliefs and the values that make us who we are. The most important stories may be those we share with family and friends, and they all help to preserve memories, explain our past, our present and help us to imagine our future.

The therapeutic effects of storytelling are well documented and research suggests that stories can help us to explore and re-interpret past life events in a gentle, non-threatening way. Stories can open our minds to more positive explanations about our previous experiences: ones with less self-blame and more hopeful resolutions.

The misconceptions that many children in care have about themselves and their lack of self-worth has been 'hard wired' into their brains. They are laid down in their unconscious memory, and attempting to access these misconceptions at a conscious level will not necessary have the desired result. Using metaphorical stories that mirror aspects of the children's lives can access these unconscious feelings and help them to challenge and reframe their negative inner beliefs.

Many traditional children's stories begin with 'Once upon a time'; there is adversity or challenge in the middle and they end with a resolution, as 'they all live happily ever after'. This familiar, tried and tested formula can be seen in fairy tales and fables. These stories can be read and enjoyed at face value, but they also contain powerful, subliminal messages. Many traditional children's stories are examples of extended metaphors. These apparently simple tales are in fact multilayered. They use metaphor as a way of reframing negative experiences into positive, resourceful outcomes.

In recent years an abundance of 'therapeutic' storybooks have been published (see children's book list). Many are specifically aimed at children who have suffered early neglect and abuse and may now be struggling with particular issues. Some are written explicitly for children in care or adopted. As with more traditional tales, these stories can be understood on many different levels and children must be allowed to take what they want from the story, and in their own time.

We all tend to find it much easier to talk about issues that affect others, as this gives us a sense of detachment. Once we personalize the story, there is a tendency to close up. You can discuss, with empathy, the frightened, sad feelings the characters in the books might have, but the stories should be read to the child, at face value, without trying to interpret them.

Indirectly these books may help the child to unravel their own perceptions and feelings about particular events. If the child wants to elaborate on the story, use this time constructively to work on those unconscious feelings, but continue to use the third person. The story is not their story, but it may have some resonance for them. They may want you to read the book many times, and without realizing it, this gradually allows them to process their own history.

When selecting suitable stories for the child, be mindful of their emotional age. Books for a younger age range may be appropriate. As their developmental age is often much younger than their chronological age, many teenagers also enjoy these simple therapeutic books.

Some children will make the connection easily and will want to discuss the theme further. Others may not recognize or acknowledge any link to their own life experiences, but those hidden messages may still be working on an unconscious level. If the child is completely disinterested in the book you have selected, just try another one, at another time.

Story time could become an enjoyable ritual. It's an opportunity for the child to begin to understand different voice tones and the accompanying facial expressions. It can be a quiet, intimate time. At the end of a life journey work session the social worker (or, at bedtime, carers or parents) may wish to use familiar calming stories that have a simple, happy ending. At other times of the day, story time could be a lively, interactive activity. The story could pose more dilemmas and difficulties for the main character, before the happy resolution is reached.

Children love routine, so having a special time or place to share stories can be beneficial. If able to accept physical contact, the child may 'cuddle in' as the book is read. For children who find intimacy and close contact difficult, just sitting beside them would be a good start. Some children find it impossible to sit still and will need to move around, touch things, stand on their heads, etc. while you read. This can be disconcerting but persevere, for they will still be taking those messages in.

Some stories lend themselves to exaggerated gestures or even roleplay. Children who've had inconsistent or neglectful parenting often have difficulty recognizing different facial expressions and their associated emotions (happy, angry, sad, frightened, etc.). Story time can begin to address such issues, in a playful and indirect way. No matter what age the child is, try exaggerating expressions as you read. Show the child your sad/happy face, or use a mirror to compare different expressions. This could also gently encourage eye contact, something that children with low self-esteem often find uncomfortable.

There are of course also many children's films that entertain and delight, and also contain powerful subliminal messages. They can be equally effective in helping children to process elements of their own story. They also use images and metaphors to tap into the child's unconscious. Creating a story specifically for the child, or telling a story by putting on a puppet show, are other options. Whatever medium is used, stories can help the child to overlay negative inner beliefs with more positive ones.

This is not a 'quick-fix' solution, but it is a gentle, indirect way of helping children gain a more realistic perspective of their past. Stories can help children explore their feelings, reduce self-blame and place responsibility for any neglect or abuse where it belongs – on the adults and not on themselves.

Child Appreciation Days

Child Appreciation Days – also referred to as Life Appreciation or Child Celebration Days – are held during the 'linking' or 'matching' process of a child with prospective adopters, before formal introductions start. They are not directly referred to in current adoption legislation, but they are considered to be good practice by many adoption agencies throughout the UK. Some local authorities have incorporated them into their permanency planning policies for both adoptive and long-term fostering placement.

Child Appreciation Days have their origins in the statutory meetings which must be held when an adoption or long-term foster placement disrupts. Disruption meetings aim to identify the reasons for the breakdown, to learn lessons from the events surrounding this, and to help professionals to determine the best possible plans for the child's future care.

Many of the adopters or carers attending these meetings found that the information shared gave them a more 'complete picture' of the child. They felt this would have been more usefully provided at the beginning of the process, rather than when the placement had ended. Some believed that had they been given this extra knowledge, prior to the child's placement, they would have been better prepared, and it might have prevented the disruption.

The Child Appreciation Days are therefore part of the preparation. They aim to provide a comprehensive view of the child and to help the prospective adopters or carers to fully appreciate him/her. Although they will already have read many reports, it is widely recognized that 'It can be difficult to gain a holistic view of the child, of who they are and what has made them who they are, as these reports are not designed to provide information in this way' (Sayers and Roach 2011, p.17). This day is an attempt to readdress this. It is an opportunity for the prospective adopters or carers 'to walk in the child's shoes'. The day brings the child 'alive' for everyone. Although the child is not usually present, he/she is the guest of honour and these events are potentially a powerful part of the child's life work.

It gives the adopters or permanent carers the opportunity to meet and hear directly from significant people in the child's life (e.g. health visitors, medical advisers, child minders, current and previous foster carers, nursery staff, teachers, former and current social workers, contact supervisors, independent reviewing officers, therapists, etc.). This is 'a unique and innovative way…of helping potential adopters not just to *read* about and *hear* information regarding their new child, but also to *see* and *meet people* who have played a part in a child's life, and to experience *feelings* about the child'. (Sayers and Roach 2011, p.17).

Birth relatives could attend part of the day, if considered appropriate, although generally meetings between adopters and birth parents are arranged separately. Such meetings can be emotionally charged and draining for all concerned, so holding them as part of the Child Appreciation Day may prove very stressful, and could detract from the main purpose of the day.

The day is all about enabling the prospective carers or adopters to develop an appreciation of the child in the context of their wider family, their early experiences both pre- and post-birth, and while in care. It's not just about drawing together a factual summary of events and significant experiences. It's a time for those involved to share photographs, videos, anecdotes and memories, both happy and sad. It should help everyone to really tune into the child on an emotional and cognitive level. It is a time to consider:

- What the child has experienced and when.

- What they may have thought or felt about what happened to them.

- The possible impact on him/her at that time and in the long term.

- The coping strategies used and any challenging behaviour.

- What those present think the child currently understands of why these things happened.

Flexibility is required regarding invites. Some participants may only be able to attend for a short while or at a particular time. Ideally the chair/facilitator should try to take the contributors chronologically through the child's life, enabling prospective adopters or carers to really process the child's journey.

A flow chart or wallpaper work can be used to plot and illustrate the child's journey. This can highlight pre-birth experiences, the birth and significant events, including number of moves and placements to date. It provides a powerful and very graphic aid for everyone present.

The chair/facilitator should ensure that the child remains the focus of the day. He/she should be able to reflect on the information given and consider what messages the child may have internalized, particularly in terms of their self-esteem and sense of self-blame. Exploring the child's attachment history, reactions to stress and coping strategies, and noting patterns in behaviour will help to prepare for the transition. It will also enable the prospective adopter or carer to begin to think about the child's immediate and future needs, and to consider appropriate re-parenting techniques to use after placement.

Such days enable prospective carers or adopters to make a well-informed decision about whether or not they feel able to parent the child effectively, and if they wish to proceed with the placement. If they do, this meeting will have provided the key to answering so many of the what, why, when and where questions that the child will continue to ask in future years.

There are resource implications, and preparing for and organizing such days requires a great deal of planning and coordinating. It is well worth the effort, and the impact and possible lifelong benefits for the child and prospective family are enormous. Sayers and Roach's guide on Child Appreciation Days contains excellent tips on planning the day and provides useful templates for letters, explanatory information that can be sent to attendees, and suggested wording for a letter to the child after the meeting. Some agencies provide a detailed report of all the information gathered for the prospective adopters or carers, and a few record or capture the contributions on video.

This day provides a unique opportunity for the prospective adopters and carers to gather and store so many of the child's experiences and memories. Happy times and shared anecdotes will not be lost for the child. In addition, a letter or a simple child-friendly record of the day can be prepared for the child to keep.

Most attendees are happy to have photographs taken and to record when and how they knew the child, to add some positive comments, their memories of the child and to wish them well for the future, before they leave the meeting. These sheets can be collated and bound or placed in an appropriate folder.

The message for the child is that they came together for this special day; they valued and cared about the child, and wanted him/her to have a positive future. Some participants may prefer to email their comments later, although having a simple handwritten contribution on the day could make this a more personal keepsake for the child.

Life story books

The life story book provides the 'coherent narrative', and should tell the child's story in an honest, sensitive and age appropriate way. The book is a legal requirement for adopted children and is now considered good practice for all children in care, especially those placed with long-term foster carers or Special Guardians.

Life story books may be the culmination of the life journey work. They are often described as the 'end product' of the work although, as life work is a lifelong process, it is never at an end. Furthermore, for some children, particularly for babies or very young children, the book is prepared and given to the adoptive parents within ten days of the court hearing celebrating the child's adoption order. In adoption, therefore, the life story book often comes first. It is the starting point. It will provide the foundation for the life journey work that must follow.

Providing long-term carers and adopters with life story books is imperative. It can be the catalyst for the healing and attachment process. Over the years, they will be able to use a truthful and carefully written book with great effect to help children revisit and reframe their early experiences. As they mature, children will continue to need help to process their history.

The book must be an honest account of the child's story. Concerns about being 'non-judgemental' and not 'apportioning blame' in relation to birth parents leads many social workers to give a very 'gentle' explanation, such as: 'Your birth mother loved you, but couldn't look after you' or 'Your birth mother wasn't well, so couldn't look after you.' These may be true statements, but they are incomplete explanation. As Sydney and Price (2014) note, such 'nebulous descriptions, although well intentioned, can obscure reality and prevent children from grappling with core truths about their developmental experiences and lives' (Sydney and Price 2014, p.19). The child must have a clear account of events and concerns.

As with life journey work, the book should contain positive subliminal messages for the child. The language used should raise the child's self-esteem and self-worth. It should strengthen their sense of being loved, valued, of belonging and of being claimed by their current family.

Strengthening the child's sense of permanency and stability and promoting healthy attachments should be a primary aim. This is best achieved by starting the book in the present and using the 'present – past – present – future' format, as advocated and explained fully by Rees (2017). This publication also contains sample books and suggested wording for children who are adopted, fostered or living with Special Guardians.

With the rise in social media, and to protect young children, most agencies now agree that copies of original birth certificates, full names and dates of birth of birth parents, addresses and any other identifying information, should generally not be included in the child's life story book. This is endorsed by government guidelines which suggest that some details 'need to be given to the child at a time when they are emotionally able to cope and understand the information. Consideration should be given on whether the surname of the birth parents, family and others should be included in the life story book' (*Adoption Statutory Guidance* 2013, AAR 35).

A life story book must be one that the child is not afraid to read. It must provide a clear narrative, so shouldn't be overloaded with too much of the life journey work: this obscures the child's story. The book must invite the child in. It should be colourful, playful and child-friendly. While providing a truthful account of earlier past events, it must help the child feel comfortable in the present and leave them with a sense of a hopeful future.

Later life letters

The provision of a later life letter is a statutory requirement for all children placed with adoptive parents. As with life story books, the completed letter should be given to the adopters within ten days of the Celebratory Adoption Hearing (*Adoption Statutory Guidance* 2013, AAR 35). These letters, giving background information, have their origins in a time when adoptions were shrouded in secrecy. Adoptive parents were given very little information about the birth family's circumstances prior to placement, other than this letter.

The original letters, referred to as 'background letters', provided basic details and a brief summary. They were addressed to and given to the adoptive parents, with the expectation that they would share the letter with the adoptee at an appropriate age. At that time, most assumed that this would be on reaching adulthood. I met several adopted adults who, as children, had known very little about the circumstances leading to their adoption. They had vivid memories of suddenly and without any preparation, being presented with their background letter, literally on their 18th birthdays.

Today, adoptive parents are given a detailed history and can access various assessment reports and other documents. The child should also have a life story book. There is an assumption that the book, the letter and other information will be shared with the child in stages and as appropriate, depending not only on the child's chronological age, but also on their cognitive abilities and emotional development and maturity.

Later life letters are usually shared sometime during adolescence. At the time of writing the letter, it would be inappropriate for the social worker to suggest a specific age, as children develop at different rates. The adoptive parents will be in the best position to make a judgment on this.

The letters are given to adoptive parents for safekeeping, as were background letters, but there is a change of focus. This is now an opportunity for the social worker to tell the young person directly about their involvement. The letter is addressed to the child, not to the adopters, and provides a more personal account. The worker can share, first hand, their memories and knowledge of the birth family.

As well as being a detailed and honest account of events, the letter may contain some 'soft' information about the birth family, descriptions and anecdotes. It should provide sufficient detail to give a clear understanding of the events leading to the adoption. The letter should enable the adoptees to dispel any fantasies they still harbour, and alert them to any risks, should they wish to initiate contact with their birth family in the future. By that stage, they need to be fully aware of potential safeguarding issues.

With the rise in social media, to protect young children and in line with statutory guidelines, most agencies are now cautious about including identifying information in the child's life story book. Others feel strongly that it is the child's right to have all of the details: full names, dates of birth of significant birth family members and addresses and include these in the book. Increasingly, however, practitioners are keeping this information for the later life letter.

Some are even more circumspect. They draw on recent neurological research, which explains why children tend to 'jump in with both feet'. The processes needed to plan and organize, referred to as 'executive functions', are still developing in the adolescent brain (Jensen 2015). Many teenagers have poor impulse control and are drawn to risk taking behaviour. This does raise questions about the wisdom of sharing potentially harmful identifying information at this stage.

Practitioners should certainly be mindful of the local authority's continued duty of care, beyond the adoption order, but most teenagers are very inquisitive. If not given these details in the letter, they may search for them on the internet. Better, perhaps, that this information is shared while the adoptive parents are there to offer guidance, support and, if necessary, protection.

Clearly there shouldn't be anything in the letter that the adoptive parents are not aware of. They need to familiarize themselves with the content, so they can judge when their child is mature enough to deal with and digest the information. By the time the young person reads the letter, there shouldn't be anything that the adopters have not already shared verbally, during the preceding years.

The later life letter 'bridges the gap' between the life story book, which is written using simple, child-friendly language, and the more detailed reports that are available should the adoptee seek access to their records in the future.

Adoption Statutory Guidance (2013) suggests that a 'social worker who knows the child, preferably the child's social worker, should prepare the later life letter. If there has been a change of social worker, then more than one worker should contribute to the letter, or there could be more than one letter. Ex-foster carers and members of the birth family can also contribute to the letter or can be encouraged to write their own. 'The child's birth family could be asked by the agency to write either their own letters to the child or could contribute to the agency's letter, should either of these steps feel appropriate (*Adoption Statutory Guidance* 2013, AAR 35).

The format is up to the social worker and, as they are quite lengthy, some prefer to divide the letter into sections. Ryan and Walker (2016) suggest as a framework:

- the reason for writing the letter

- information about the child at birth

- information about birth parents

- details of birth parents' relationship

- an explanation of why the child was adopted

- and ending the letter with information about the agency and accessing records.

Whatever structure is preferred, the letter should use language that is appropriate for an adolescent or young adult rather than a young child (e.g. refer to the adopters as 'your parents' or 'your mum' or 'your dad' rather than, as I have often seen, 'your mummy' or 'your daddy'). This is an official letter, so should not be on pink paper or decorated with borders of stars or flowers. You may be thinking of the toddler you have recently placed, but he/she will be a young man or woman by the time the letter is read. It should be printed on headed paper with the adoption agency's address and other contact details clearly displayed, dated and signed by the author.

The British Agency for Adoption and Fostering's Good Practice Guide (Moffat 2012) is helpful and contains sample letters and suggested wording for explaining difficult and painful issues. Moffat recommends warning the young person early in the letter that it may be difficult to read, as it contains information that could be upsetting. Hopefully the adoptee will already be aware of all of the information in the letter before reading it. While seeing sensitive information written down may have a big impact, we should be cautious about pre-empting reactions. For some it could provide a welcome and positive validation of their memories, and confirmation of the information that has already been openly shared with them.

I have included a covering letter for adoptive parents (Appendix C) and a sample later life letter for the child (Appendix D). Although the circumstances and content of the later life letters will vary, the opening and closing paragraphs could be similar for all children. The covering letter endorses the adopters' continuous role in life work. It reinforces the expectation that they will use the life story book and gradually build on the information it contains, so there will be no surprises when their child eventually reads the letter. It also reminds the adopters that they can seek further advice from the local authority about sharing the letter.

The later life letter is also an opportunity to give the adoptee information about the adoption agency. It explains that they can make contact for advice or support at any stage in the future. They can also access adoption records when they are 18 years old. If they would like further information before this, they should be advised to speak to their adoptive parents first. With the adopters' agreement, many teenagers access their records earlier. A copy of the later life letter is retained on the adoption records. (Adoption records must be securely stored and retained by the adoption agency for 100 years.)

Contact

Facilitating regular contact between children in care and members of their birth families is considered to be good practice. The Children and Families Act 2014 permits local authorities to refuse contact if they believe there are safeguarding issues, or if it does not promote the child's welfare, but generally contact is promoted by social care agencies, and directed by the judiciary. This is particularly so in the early weeks and months of the child coming into care. It is seen to be of benefit and as having positive consequences: maintaining family relationships, easing the child and birth family's sense of separation and loss, reassuring the child that the birth relative still exists and is well.

Contact also provides an opportunity for the supervising worker to observe the quality of care provided and to begin to assess the nature of the attachment relationship. This informs future care plans. Following this period of assessment, the child may return home and continued contact should make their period in care less traumatic and the transition easier.

Some children remain in care and move on to permanent fostering or adoptive placements, and contact plans will be reviewed. At this stage, direct contact with birth family members may be reduced. In some instances it ceases altogether, or indirect contact may be arranged.

Indirect contact, referred to as 'postbox', 'letterbox' or 'information exchange', is a confidential mailing service, organized by the agency responsible for placing the child. It involves the exchange of letters or cards, and sometimes photographs, between members of the birth family and the child's carers or adopters. In a few instances it includes recordings or videos.

Contact, whether direct or indirect, can make an important contribution to life work. It keeps the lines of communication open between the birth family, child and substitute families. It provides opportunities to check details with the birth family and to gather more information. This could increase the child's understanding of their history and may 'promote a sense and understanding of their own identity' (Sydney and Price 2014, p.18). In some instances, contact is a 'reality check' for the child, dispelling fantasies about the possibility of returning to live with the birth family.

Some birth parents are not able to share vital information with the agency at the time of the child's placement, e.g. name of the birth father. If there is ongoing communication, they may do this, months or even years later, when it is clear this is something the child needs, rather than 'the authority'.

Many birth parents 'move on' with their lives. They reflect on events that led to their child being removed and can accept responsibility for this. Some offer explanations and acknowledge the harm or hurt they caused and can apologize to the child. Hearing 'sorry' can authenticate the child's experiences and reduce self-blame. It could prove a powerful catalyst for the healing process to begin.

Contact may also include telephone or Skype calls, text or email correspondence. This type of contact can be difficult to monitor. With the rise in social media, it is likely that, whatever the original agreement, contact could be initiated in unforeseen and unmediated ways. This may be by the birth family or by the child.

Any contact that is not monitored or supported can have a negative effect on the child. The child's needs are constantly changing, so arrangements cannot be set 'in tablets of stone'. Arrangements appropriate for a pre-school child may not be right for a teenager. Many contacts are not reviewed, and continue for years despite causing anxiety and possibly compounding the damage the child has already suffered.

Loxterkamp (2009) challenged the widely accepted belief that contact is 'in the child's best interest'. He was concerned about the impact of contact on 'children who have suffered maltreatment at the hands of their birth parents'. He refers to the torment children can suffer when contact is superficial, and traumatic experiences are glossed over and not validated. When the child's early experiences are not acknowledged or birth parents minimize their abusive and violent behaviour, contact 'can itself be harmful and is likely to cause enduring emotional and psychological damage, even when it appears to be going well or well enough'.

Contact is a significant aspect of life work. It can be a valuable experience for the child, but Loxterkamp's research is a stark reminder of the potential harm it causes if not carefully facilitated and monitored. All parties involved: the child, birth family and substitute carers need support to ensure that contact is a positive and meaningful experience. The child may want help to think about any questions he/she has and how to express them. The birth relative may welcome advice about how he/she should respond. The carer or adopter needs to be involved to provide security, reassurance and comfort for the child. The facilitator provides structure and supports everyone.

Adoption and care records

Since the Adoption Act 1976, adopted adults (i.e. over 18 years, or over 16 years in Scotland) have had the right to apply for information that will enable them to obtain a copy of their original birth certificates. For those adopted before 12 November 1975, when adoptions were closed and shrouded in secrecy, a counselling interview is compulsory. After this date, the adoptee can apply for a copy of their birth certificate without counselling.

Anyone wishing to seek further information about their birth family, and to learn more about the circumstances surrounding their adoption, can also apply for access to their adoption records. Local authorities provide a counselling service for this, and most have social workers that specialize in this area of work. The counsellor will try to locate and access adoption records and will support, advise and sensitively guide adoptees throughout this process.

Some early adoptions were organized via third parties, often General Practitioners or local vicars. Most involved charitable organizations: these were generally affiliated to religious faiths. Although many closed years ago, with a few exceptions, their adoption records were meticulously retained and are still available.

To the 'untrained' eye, these old paper files look thin and insignificant. For the adopted adult, they are a treasure trove. Every detail they contain is valued. The impact of a handwritten letter or just a scrap of paper signed by the birth mother is immense. For many, accessing these files is the start of a very emotional journey of self-discovery. Having read her records at the age of 70, a lady I counselled had a very successful, happy reunion with her very elderly birth mother. Her questions were answered. As emphasized many times, life work is indeed a lifelong process.

Until the 1960s, some local authorities only kept adoption records for about ten years. Now, they must be retained for 100 years, from the date of the Adoption Order. There is also statutory guidance on the storage of these files. They must be archived in a secure, flood and fireproof facility and a logging system, to enable easy retrieval by authorized personnel, is essential.

Currently, for recent adoptions, there are likely to be paper files and electronic records. Some adoptees will already have read their later life or background letter. If not, a copy will be on the file. The letter provides a comprehensive summary and is a good starting point, prior to looking at other information.

At the time of placement, the adoptive parent is given a copy of Child's Permanence Report (CPR, and previously called Form E). This report gives a more detailed account of the circumstances surrounding the adoption. It contains information about all known members of the birth family, including siblings, full names, dates of birth or deaths, ethnicity, religion, occupations, addresses, significant events, chronologies and genograms. There may also be photographs of the birth parents and any siblings.

Some adoptive parents share this report with their children. Others prefer to wait until adoptees seek access to their records. Whether or not they have already seen the CPR, going through it with an adoption counsellor is advisable. It provides an opportunity for further discussion, to address any misunderstandings and to answer any queries. Retelling, reframing and processing the story continues.

Some adoptees hope to make direct contact with members of the birth family. The counsellor's role is still to offer guidance, advice and support. They can help the adoptee to think through the implications, weigh up any risks and consider the best way of making this approach. Some agencies also offer an intermediary service.

The counsellor can use some discretion when deciding what information to share. Reports prepared for the court cannot be released, unless permission has been obtained. Care must also be taken not to disclose third party information, unless this is relevant to the adoptee's understanding of their history. Adoption legislation, and the adoptee's right to know, takes precedence over the Data Protection Act 1998. Redactions are generally kept to a minimum in adoption records.

Children with 'sufficient understanding and maturity', and adults who have been in care, can also apply for access to personal information held by Children's Services. Those who spent the majority of their childhoods in care may have had multiple placements and little stability. Their lives and memories become particularly fragmented. Life work to help them unravel their confusing histories may not have been available, or disregarded by them, while in care. At a later stage many are eager to fill in the gaps in their lives. One care leaver commented that accessing this information 'gives you the confidence to talk about who you are, because it makes more sense to you' (Williams 2014).

For many post-care adults, however, trying to access records has proved a frustrating process. Some discover that their information has been lost or destroyed. The sadness, anger and resentment this causes is understandable. Prior to the 1980s, care records were often only kept for around ten years, after the child left care. Now, they must be retained for 75 years from the child's date of birth.

Unlike adoption records, the information given to care leavers is subject to the Data Protection Act 1998. They are entitled to receive *their* information, but not personal information recorded about anyone else, so limited third party details. This creates some confusion and complications for those responsible for preparing the records for viewing. Fearing litigation, some local authorities err on the side of caution and all third party information is removed.

The Care Leavers Association has campaigned for years to improve this service. They found examples of records that 'were rendered virtually meaningless by the thick black lines of redaction'. One commented that reading the file 'was difficult enough, and unexplained redactions only made it worse' (Williams 2014). Instead of filling the gaps in their lives, such experiences leave more uncertainty and unanswered questions. Details of the birth family and a clear account of early experiences are central to understanding one's history and gaining a sense of genetic identity. Unless there is risk of serious physical or emotional harm, either to the care leaver or someone else, then it is hard to see how information that helps in this process can be regarded as 'third party'.

Post-care adults deserve the same level of service as adopted adults. Preparing and sharing care records requires as much attention and sensitivity as adoption records. Care leavers may not welcome 'counselling', believing this is akin to psychotherapy. It actually refers to assistance and guidance and should be offered to all care leavers. Many may not want this and prefer information to be sent through the post, so there will be little opportunity to prepare them for the content. Nevertheless, some care leavers are particularly vulnerable and may be receiving information that is new and distressing, so support should be available. As another post-care adult found: 'The whole exercise was very emotional and quite disorientating' (Williams 2014).

Care records are arranged in numerous sections, and reports contain legal references and social work terminology. They can be confusing to read and information is not organized in a way that provides the 'coherent narrative' needed. A summary or covering letter, similar to a later life letter, would be good practice and could provide this narrative.

Those responsible for processing requests for access to care records have a particularly complex task and one requiring copious skills. In one local authority, a data protection manager charged with this role observed that it requires the post holder to be 'a hybrid between a data protection officer and a bit of a social worker or counsellor' (Williams 2014).

Adoption and care records provide the final aspect of life work. As Children's Services continue to move towards paperless offices, there are implications for practice in relation to the retention of records. With advances in technology and IT systems requiring frequent updates or replacements, tracing and accessing an individual's electronic records could prove more difficult in the future. Local authorities have a legal and moral duty to ensure that the histories and life experiences of children in their care are not lost, and that appropriate support services are in place for those requesting information in future years.

CHAPTER 6

Summing Up

At its heart, life work is storytelling. It's about helping children to know and to understand their personal stories and the life experiences that have shaped them. No two children's stories will be the same, but all contain some common themes of sadness, loss and separations, and often neglect, abuse and fear.

Life stories are frequently painful and difficult to tell, but it is the sharing and interpretation that is significant and therapeutic. 'Stories are important. Yet it is not the events themselves that matter so much but rather the way we make sense of them' (Fitzhardinge 2008). Children need a clear and honest account of their history, explained sensitively and in ways that do not inadvertently intensify the feelings of self-blame and shame. In the telling, we must always be mindful of the unwanted subliminal messages.

Practitioners must acquaint themselves with each individual story and spend time observing and listening to the child. To fully appreciate and to tune into the child's inner world, previous experiences must then be considered within the context of the theoretical framework: child development, attachment theory and neuroscience.

Life work is a complex and multilayered task and not one that an individual worker can achieve alone. It is said that 'it takes a whole village to raise a child'. To help the child in care, it takes a whole team. Enabling the child to reach his/her potential and achieve the best possible outcome is the common goal. The child needs help to assimilate difficult and distressing past experiences, while feeling safe and comfortable in the present. This is best achieved by collaboration and respect for the diverse skills and different contributions that members of the team around the child can provide.

For those working within local authorities, an appreciation of the different roles and different aspects of life work is the key to improving the quality and effectiveness of this intervention. Many consider direct life journey work to be the most important aspect of this work, as it enables the child to process and internalize their story. However, other aspects (e.g. memory books, photograph albums, life story books) are as significant. They are not only 'end products'. On the contrary, they are effective and powerful ways of layering and reinforcing the narrative of the child's life. They are of equal importance and all contribute to the processing of the story. The narrative can be told and retold from different perspectives and, as the child matures, the process of reframing and internalizing their experiences continues, often into adulthood.

By valuing and combining all aspects of life work, the practitioner will help the child to understand their story in a way that raises their sense of self-worth and self-esteem, and promotes healing and resolution. Those working in Children's Services cannot change the child's past, but they can help to reframe it, so that it does not dominate the present or dictate the future.

These suggested headings can be adapted to suit the child. Answers provided by birth parent or carer could be collated and presented as a booklet.

ALL ABOUT

(Child's Name)

Information for Foster Carers, Special Guardians or Adopters

TO BE COMPLETED PRIOR TO CHILD'S MOVE.

Child's name:

Any nicknames:

Date of birth:

Information provided by:

Date this information given:

Current placement

Child currently living with:

Relationship to child:

What does the child call you?

Do you live in a flat or house?

Is this in an urban or rural area?

How long has the child lived with you?

Who else is in the household?

Any family pets?

How would you describe the child, physically and temperamentally?

Child's typical day

Waking up

What time does the child usually wake up?

Does she wake naturally and if not, how do you wake her?

What sort of mood is she usually in on waking?

Does she wash or dress straight away or does she have breakfast first?

What does she like to do before or after breakfast (e.g. play, watch TV, read)?

On weekdays, does she go straight off to school or nursery after breakfast?

Washing

Can she wash herself? If not, how much help or supervision is needed?

Can she clean her teeth? If not, how much help or supervision is needed?

Does she prefer a bath or a shower?

What is the usual bath/shower time: morning or evening?

Can she bath or shower herself? If not, how much help or supervision is needed?

Does she like having her hair washed? If not, how do you manage this?

Do you dry her hair with a hairdryer?

Does she need any special skin care products?

Is she allergic to any products or shampoos?

Do you use a particular soap, bubble bath or body wash?

Does she enjoy having toys, bubbles or oils in the bath?

Dressing

Can she dress herself unaided? If not, please say what help is needed.

How long does it usually take her to dress?

What does she like wearing?

Does she like to choose what to wear?

Can she do buttons, use zips, manage buckles or tie laces?

Feeding

Can she feed herself? If not, how do you feed her?

Does she have a high chair or need a booster or special seat?

Does she use a spoon or can she use a knife and fork?

Is her food minced or liquidised?

What does she use to drink: a cup, glass, bottle, special feeder?

Does she usually wear a bib, if so what type?

Does she have any special dietary requirements, if so what?

Is she allergic to anything?

What are her favourite foods and drinks?

What does she dislike?

Does she have a big or small appetite?

If she has a packed lunch, what do you usually put in it?

Does she have extra snacks, treats or drinks during the day? If so, what?

What do you call your main meals and what time do you have them? (e.g. breakfast, brunch, lunch, tea, dinner or supper)

Toileting

Is she toilet trained?

Does she wear nappies during the day and/or at night? If so, what size and type?

Does she go to the toilet when needed?

Does she need any help?

Can she let you know you when she needs to go?

What words or signs does she use?

Are there any particular times when she expects to be taken to the toilet?

Does she use the toilet during the night and, if so, does she need help with this?

Do you leave a light on for her?

Are there any particular toileting concerns?

Evening time

What does she like to do in the evening and what doesn't she like?

Does she have any favourite TV programmes?

Is there anything on TV that frightens her?

Bedtime

What time does she start to get tired and what time does she usually go to bed?

Does she have a nap during the day If so, when, where and for how long?

What is the usual bedtime routine and how long does this take?

Does she sleep in a cot or a bed?

Does she enjoy bedtime stories? If so, does she have favourite ones?

Does she enjoying reading before going to sleep or listening to music?

Does she take a drink to bed? If so, what and in what container?

Does she sleep in her own room or share?

Does she like to get ready for bed and then join you for a while before bedtime?

Does she like to be carried to bed?

Does she like the door open or shut, and does she like the curtains/blinds closed?

Does she take any toys to bed?

Is there a special toy or comforter? Does it have a pet name?

What sort of bedding does she have?

Does she like to be tucked in tightly or loosely?

How does she sleep? Is she restless?

Does she usually settle and fall asleep quite quickly?

Are you aware of her having any dreams or nightmares?

Does she ever wet or soil the bed?

Does she get up in the night for any reason? If so, what for?

Does she ever sleepwalk?

Is she frightened of the dark?

Does she have a nightlight? If so, where?

Other information

Nursery/school

Does she attend nursery/school? If so, where and how often?

How does she get there (e.g. walk, car, bus, cycle)?

Are there any problems getting her there?

What does she like most and least about nursery/school?

Is she usually happy, quiet, sad or anxious there?

What, if anything, causes her difficulties or worries at nursery/school?

Is there a particular teacher or member of staff she likes?

Does she have any special friends there? What are their first names?

Does she usually have homework? If so how much and does she need help with this?

Activities

What activities, games or toys does she like?

Does she prefer playing alone, with other children or with adults?

Does she like outdoor activities (e.g. cycling, football, skateboarding) or does she prefer indoor activities (e.g. jigsaws, painting, computer games), or both?

Does she belong to any clubs or activity groups?

Does she have any regular daytime activities?

Does she have any hobbies or collections?

Travelling

Does she like travelling by car?

Does she suffer from travel sickness? If so, is there anything that helps to relieve this?

Do you know if she has been on a train, bus, boat or aeroplane?

Behaviour

Does she display any concerning or challenging behaviour?

How do you know if she is worried or upset about something?

Does she become quiet, tearful, withdrawn, grumpy, angry or are there other signs?

Are you aware of any particular situations that trigger worrying behaviour?

How do you manage any difficulties that occur?

Is she able to relate to other children and to adults?

How does she respond to new visitors to the home or to strangers outside?

Speech

Do you have concerns about her language development?

If so, does she have speech therapy or has a referral been made?

If already started, with whom and how often?

Are you able to understand her? Can others understand her?

Rather than words, does she use other ways of communicating?

Does she use any special words or pet names for things? If so, what are they?

Medical

Are there any ongoing medical concerns or health issues?

Are there any regular doctor or hospital appointments? Is she having any specialist input?

Please give details, including date of last appointment and date of next.

Has she had any hospital admissions that you are aware of?

Does she have any regular medication?

Does she suffer from frequent colds, chest infections, ear or throat infections?

Any allergies or other medical conditions?

When was her last dental check-up and did she need any treatment?

Additional needs

Does she have any physical or learning disabilities? If so, give details.

Does she wear spectacles, contact lenses, hearing aids or use a walking frame or wheelchair?

Is she willing to use them and do these aids cause any discomfort?

What impact do the disabilities have?

How do you manage the child's additional needs?

Are there specialist services involved to help her and to support you?

General development

Does she have any developmental delays, physically or cognitively? If so is this in a specific area (e.g. speech) or is it global delay?

What impact does this have on everyday life for her and for you?

Does she need any special adaptations?

What other services are involved and are you providing anything special to help her?

Animals

Does she have any contact with animals, if so what ones?

Is she frightened of and are you aware of her ever being hurt by an animal?

Is she allergic to any animals?

Sensory information

Do you use a particular brand of washing powder, fabric conditioner, soap, bubble bath, shampoo or creams for the child?

Is a particular perfume or aftershave used by main carers or by birth parent? (This could trigger happy, sad or frightening memories.)

Does she use a comforter or a special cuddly toy or blanket when upset?

How is her bedroom decorated? What colour?

Are you aware of any everyday sounds that she might find soothing or frightening? (e.g. songs, nursery rhymes, theme music, running water, police siren, dogs barking, etc.)

Memories

Do you have any funny memories of things that the child said or did while living with you?

Further information:

The information you supply will help to make the transition as smooth as possible for the child.

Please add anything else it would be helpful for those responsible for her future care to know.

Appendix B

Why did I come into care?

Different people may have different views and say different things:

My name:

Today's date:

I came into care on:

My social worker said:

My mum said:

My other relatives said:

My foster carer said:

The judge said:

I think I came into care because:

More activity sheets can be downloaded from:
www.thejoyoflifework.com

Appendix C

Covering letter to adopters about Later Life Letter

Agency name

Address

Date

Dear

Please find enclosed a copy of the Later Life Letter prepared for Harry. You also have his Life Story Book, and reading this will help him to understand something of his early history. Over the years, you can build on the information in his book, and I hope that you will be able to answer any questions he has as they arise, and as his level of understanding increases.

The Later Life Letter contains further details about Harry's birth parents and early life. It is important that you read the letter and keep it safe, until you feel that Harry is ready to read and digest the content. A copy is also retained on his adoption records.

Most adoptive parents share this letter during the adolescent years, but you know your child and will be in the best position to judge when Harry is ready. I hope that you will discuss the content of this letter with him verbally over the years, so that when he actually reads it, the information is not completely new for him.

In view of the rise in social media, many adoption agencies are now more cautious about including identifying information in these letters. But I do not feel, in this instance, Harry's birth parents pose any particular risks so, as you will see, I have included their surnames and year of birth. I have not however included specific addresses or dates of birth. These details are in other reports you have, and you can share these with Harry, should he request them, and when you feel it is appropriate. Should he then wish to use this information to initiate contact with members of his birth family, he can do so with your guidance and support.

I would advise that you give Harry the letter before he reaches the age of 18 years, as at that time he may apply for access to his adoption records. If you have already shared the letter, you will have prepared him for this.

Please remember that you can contact this agency's Adoption Support Service, or the one in your local authority, if you need further advice about how and when to share this letter, or any other issues, at any time in the future.

I wish you and your family all the best.

Yours sincerely,

Joy Rees
Social Worker
Looked After Children's Team

Appendix D

Sample Later Life Letter for young person

Agency name

Address

Date

Dear Harry

I doubt that you will actually remember me, although your parents may have told you something about my involvement, before your adoption. There is also a photograph of me in your life story book, taken with you and your mum and dad, outside the court, on the day of your Adoption Celebratory Hearing.

I was working as a social worker for this authority, in the 'Looked After Children's Team', when you were born, when you were fostered and when you first went to live with your mum and dad. My team was responsible for finding permanent substitute families for children who were not able to stay with their birth families. You initially had a social worker called Paul, and then Sharon. I became involved when Sharon left the department. I first met you in your foster home, when you were about six months old.

You probably read your Life Story Book many times when you were younger, so already know something of your history.

Over the years, your parents may have given you more information, and I hope that they have been able to answer most of your questions as they arose. As I knew you when you were a baby and I met your birth parents, Sally and Alan, I also want to share some of my memories with you, and to tell you what happened before you came to live with your parents.

Sally and Alan

Your birth mother, Sally Lopez, met your birth father, Alan Driscoll, sometime in 2010, when they were both around 19 years old. Sally was born in Chessington, Surrey, in 1991 and later moved with her family to Croydon in South London. She was a lively, outgoing and talkative lady. She was quite tall and of average build: about 5ft 8in and 10 stone, with size 6 feet. She had long dark brown hair, brown eyes and an olive complexion.

Sally usually wore casual clothes: t-shirts, jumpers, jeans or leggings. She liked listening to pop music and watching television. Her favourite programmes were the soaps, like *Eastenders* and *Coronation Street*. She also liked *Dr Who* and loved Harry Potter films.

Sally went to Croydon Girls School. She didn't enjoy school and left before taking any exams, at 16 years of age. She worked as a shelf filler, and later on the tills in a supermarket. This is where Alan first met her.

Alan was born in 1990 and was quieter than Sally. He worked in a garage in Croydon, and the supermarket was just around the corner. He went there to buy something to eat at lunchtimes. Sally said that his usual lunch was a ham and pickle sandwich, a packet of smoky bacon crisps and a can of Coke! He would always make a point of going to Sally's till to pay, instead of using the self-service. It took him a few weeks, but he eventfully plucked up the courage to ask her out.

Alan was tall and slim, with blue eyes and dark curly hair, which he usually kept very short. Sometimes he had a beard. He was 6ft with size 12 feet. Like Sally, he tended to wear casual clothes, mainly sweatshirts, jeans, tracksuits and trainers. He liked repairing old cars, playing computer games and watching action films and thrillers.

Sally had spent all of her childhood in South London, while Alan was from Liverpool and he had a strong Liverpudlian accent. He moved from there to London when he was 18 years old. He said that there were no jobs in his home town, so he came south looking for work.

At first Sally and Alan felt that they were very happy and, after knowing each other for a month or so, they decided to live together. They rented a flat in Raynes Park, south-west London. Unfortunately, their relationship soon became strained and they began arguing quite a lot, mainly about money. They fell behind on their rent and were threatened with eviction.

Alan said that he had been drinking heavily since his early teens, and he knew that he was now beginning to rely on alcohol too much. He thought that it helped him to feel less stressed. Sally didn't drink as much, but it soon became apparent that they were both using various illegal drugs. This meant even less money to pay the rent and for other essentials, and their relationship became more volatile.

Although Alan came across as a placid, quiet person, there was another side to him. Under pressure he could became quite an angry young man, and there were several episodes of domestic violence. Alan often lost his temper, usually after drinking, and on several occasions he hurt Sally quite badly. She was often seen with bruises and black eyes, and on one occasion she had a broken nose. At the time she said that they were just accidents, and she remained committed to Alan.

By the middle of 2011 they had both lost their jobs. Their lives had become very disorganised and they were often late for work, or on some days they didn't turn up at all. In August of that year, Alan also received a short prison sentence for several offences of theft. He was also charged with assaulting Sally, although this charge was later dropped.

Despite all of their difficulties, when Sally and Alan realised that they were going to have a baby they were delighted and started to plan for your birth. They made an effort to put more order into their lives. Sally attended her prenatal appointments, they cleaned up their flat and tried hard to reduce their drinking and drug taking. Staff at the Drug and Alcohol Dependency Unit became involved and they both started a detoxification programme. This is when Paul, a social worker with the Referral and Assessment Team, became involved.

Sally and Alan's childhood

Neither of your birth parents had very stable childhoods, and received no support from their families. Knowing more about their respective histories might help you to have more of an understanding of them and their circumstances.

Alan was an only child and his mother, Elaine, was a single parent. He had never known his birth father. He said Elaine hadn't been able to tell him anything about him, not even his name, and this is something that Alan had always found very hard to accept. He remained angry that his mother wouldn't, or couldn't, give him any more information.

When younger, his maternal grandmother had been very involved in his care. Alan and Elaine lived with her, and he remembered this as the happiest time of his life. He was devastated when his grandmother died suddenly, following a heart attack, when he was eight years old. He said that his life changed after this. His mother was an only child and he has never known any other members of his extended family, so it was now just him and Elaine.

During his early teens, Elaine experienced mental health problems and she was often admitted to hospital suffering from depression. Alan remembered several short and unhappy periods in care with different foster carers. As he became older he felt that he was, more or less, left to fend for himself.

Alan said that he enjoyed school when he was younger, and when his grandmother was alive, although he always found reading hard and remembers having some extra help with this. During his teens his behaviour at school became more disruptive and he recalled having lots of detentions, usually for fighting with other pupils. He struggled to keep up with the work, had poor school attendance and said he just 'dropped out' when he was 15 years old, and left officially at 16 years without any formal qualifications.

He worked in a warehouse and then secured a job at a garage as a trainee mechanic, but lost this job after a few months. This is when he decided to move away from Liverpool. He was proud of his northern roots and said that he would always be a 'Scouser', and remained a loyal supporter of Liverpool Football Club. His mother was still living in Liverpool, but he hadn't had any contact with her since he left the area. He believed that she didn't care about him, and was just relieved when he left home.

Sally's childhood was also a difficult one. She was the eldest of five girls – one born every year after her. She felt that her parents had never had a happy relationship, and as a young child she remembered lots of shouting and arguing. She witnessed many incidents of domestic violence as she was growing up. Sally described her father, Anton, who was originally from Spain, as 'a big loud bully'. Sally said that she looked like her father, but hadn't inherited his temperament. Her mother, Marie, was a Londoner. She was the quiet, timid one and most of Anton's anger, usually when he had been drinking, was directed at her.

At times, her father had also physically assaulted Sally. On one occasion, when she was about 14 years old, she stepped in to protect her mother and this resulted in Sally having a broken arm. At the time she told everyone that she had fallen over.

The family was well known to the children's services and, for a while, Sally and her siblings where on the 'at risk' register. Despite all the concerns however, Sally was never actually put in care herself, although her two youngest siblings lived with foster carers for a while.

When Sally was in her teens, Marie was diagnosed with ovarian cancer, and sadly she died when Sally was 17 years old. Sally left home a few months after this, because she felt she couldn't go on living in the same house as her father, and wasn't prepared to put up with his temper any longer. She was already working in the supermarket at that time, and rented a room in a local hostel. Although her father and sisters still lived in Croydon, she had very little contact with any of them. She said that her father's drinking had increased since her mother's death and her sisters had their own 'problems'. None of them were in a position to support her.

Your birth

You were born on Monday 15 October 2012 at 2.35pm in West London Hospital. Alan was at your birth and said that he just fell in love with you as soon as you were born. They both registered your birth and gave you the name of Harry, after Harry Potter. You had the same surname as Alan, Driscoll, and his name is on your original birth certificate.

You arrived a month earlier than expected. It was a quick labour and normal birth. Sally said that she only just made it to the hospital in time and you were almost born in the ambulance. You weighed just 2.26kgs (5lbs) and were 45cm (just under 18in) long. This is quite small for a newborn, partly due to you arriving so early.

You remained in the special baby unit for the first few weeks of your life. You had some breathing difficulties and needed extra oxygen and, as Sally had still been using illegal drugs during part of her pregnancy, this affected you. You tested positive, and had treatment for ten days, for a condition called neonatal abstinence syndrome. This is basically the same as drug withdrawal symptoms in an adult, so incredibly painful and unpleasant for a tiny baby. You were very poorly in those early days.

While you were still in hospital everyone involved, health and social care professionals, were very concerned about you and your birth parents' situation. They didn't believe that they would be able to care for you consistently and safely because of the nature and extent of their own personal difficulties and addictions. A Family Group Conference was arranged. This was a meeting with your birth parents and everyone else involved. Usually members of the extended birth family attend these meetings, to see if there is anyone else in a position to provide care for you. As Sally and Alan were both estranged from their respective families, there was no one else.

Sally and Alan clearly loved you. They visited you on the special baby unit every day, and wanted to take you home, but they were just not in a position to do this. They still had problems with drink and drugs and their flat was described as 'filthy and chaotic'. It would not have been a safe place for a newborn baby. Anyone who went to the flat commented on the amount of rubbish, dirty clothes, empty beer cans, bottles and drug paraphernalia lying around. Some felt the place was completely uninhabitable.

Everyone felt that you could not possibly live there, and that it would be better for you to be cared for by a foster family while long-term plans were considered. Family court proceedings were started, so that a judge could eventually decide what was best for your future. On 8 December 2012, the judge granted an Interim Care Order and this meant that Paul could now make arrangements for you to live with foster carers while long-term plans were considered.

Living with foster carers, Sam and Mark

By 15 December 2012 you had put on some weight and the doctors felt that you were well enough to leave hospital, so you were discharged and moved to your foster carers, Sam and Mark. They lived in Mitcham, South London. Before this, Sam had been to the hospital several times to meet you and had spoken to the nurses and doctors about the special care you needed. You had your first Christmas at the foster home and it was just after this that Sharon, a social worker for the Looked After Children's Team, became involved. You continued to live with your foster carers until you moved to your adoptive parent's home in September 2013.

You were still a little poorly when you first moved to the foster home. You had some feeding difficulties and your development was a little delayed. The doctors felt that this was partly because you were born prematurely, but they were also concerned about the impact of the drugs that Sally had taken while she was pregnant. For about the first four months of life you found it very hard to settle down or to achieve a sense of calm. You were often a bit irritable and agitated and, if you did manage to settle, it was usually for a short period of time – one or two hours at the most. You would also become distressed when feeds ended and you could cry for long periods. All of this is fairly typical of babies who have been subjected to illegal drugs while in the womb, and suffer withdrawal difficulties.

Sam and Mark understood this and they were very patient and worked hard to comfort and soothe you. Their own children, Jake and Fred, who were in their early teens at that time, were also very good with you and would cuddle and rock you in the evenings while they watched TV. Gradually, the situation started to ease. You began sleeping though the night and your appetite improved.

I became your social worker in April 2013, when you were six months old, and by then you were more settled. I remember admiring those big brown eyes and that lovely olive complexion, just like Sally's, and you had your first two front bottom teeth. You started crawling when you were eight months old, and then a whole new world opened up for you! One minute you were there and then whoosh! Off you went. You were rarely still. You liked to play with brightly coloured plastic cars and trucks, and enjoyed pushing them across the floor of the foster carers' living room.

Sally and Alan continued to see you while you were in foster care, although they didn't always manage to get to all of the contact sessions on time or together. A member of staff from this authority, usually Leonie, who also worked in the Looked After Team, supervised this arrangement. They usually saw you at the Children's Centre and you will have seen some photographs in your album and in your life story book of these meetings. When they came, they were so happy to see you and they were both always gentle and playful with you.

Your birth parents continued to try to sort out their difficulties and still hoped to look after you. In fact, the judge delayed making a final decision about your future care because he felt that they should be given a further chance to look after you. He also wanted to make sure that they had good legal advice and he asked for an independent assessment report on them.

In April 2013, they both started another detoxification and rehabilitation programme to help them come off – and hopefully stay off – alcohol and illegal drugs. Although it was clear that they loved you, it was also apparent that, at that time, they found it too difficult to recover from their addictions. By May 2013 they had withdrawn completely from the programme. They stayed together but their lives became more chaotic. They missed several contact sessions and when they did attend the contact supervisor noted that they often looked 'unkempt and a bit smelly'.

Alan was back in prison a month later, this time for burglary, and although Sally continued to fight very hard for your care, she found it too hard and tests taken for court showed that she was still using illegal substances.

Court proceedings

The court proceedings concerning your future care began shortly after your birth, but didn't finish until 5 June 2013, as the judge wanted to make sure your birth parents – your mother in particular – had been given enough support and time on the detoxification programme.

The final hearing was at the West London Family Proceedings Court. Lots of information was gathered, assessments were completed and numerous reports compiled about you, your birth parents and members of your extended family. A Children's Guardian – who is someone independent of the court and Children's Services – also visited you and spoke to your birth parents and others involved and she prepared another report for the court. Basically, everyone agreed that Sally and Alan would not be able to provide the care you needed. There were important decisions to be made and the judge had to consider everything very carefully, which is why it took such a long time.

Your birth parents attended the court hearings every day throughout the hearings. Alan was escorted from High Down Prison each day. Sally asked for more time to deal with her addictions, but by this time the judge felt that she had already been given plenty of opportunities and, as you were getting older, you needed to be settled. At that time, Sally was still not looking after herself very well, so she just wouldn't have been able to look after you.

Finally, the judge said that it would be best for you to live with a new family – one where you could have a happy and secure childhood and remain until you reached adulthood: an adoptive family. Understandably, Sally and Alan were very disappointed, upset and angry about this decision.

The judge granted a Full Care Order and a Placement Order, and this gave the local authority permission to place you with prospective adoptive parents. Before this happened, Sally saw you to say farewell on 7 August 2013, and you saw Alan on 15 August 2013. It was an emotional time for both of them and again you have some photographs of these contacts in your album.

Your adoption

I worked with Anne – a social worker in the Adoption Team – and together we went to see several prospective adoptive parents. We both felt that Mary and Brian would be the best parents for you. I first met them at the end of June 2013, at their home. They had heard all about you from their adoption worker, and really hoped that you would be able to live with them. They knew that you had been unwell when first born and that there had been concerns about your birth parents' substance misuse and uncertainties around the long-term impact this may have on you. They met with the medical adviser to discuss this further and were very relaxed and open-minded about the future – and you needed parents just like that. Everyone thought that they had plenty of energy and understanding and would be good, loving parents for you.

They also met your foster carers and heard more about you, and learnt about your daily routine and likes and dislikes: you loved bananas but didn't like apples; you loved bathtime but didn't like bedtime; you loved being taken for walks in your buggy, but didn't like the car seat.

The Adoption and Permanency Panel came next. This Panel is made up of social workers and people who have been fostered or adopted themselves, and also someone who has already adopted children. The panel members read all the reports about you and about your parents and, on 3 August 2013, they recommended that Mary and Brian would be great parents for you. A week later the Head of Social Care, who was also the Agency Decision Maker, agreed this.

Your mum and dad were very relieved, happy and excited. They were also able to meet Sally. This was a very emotional but positive experience for everyone. Sally phoned me afterwards and said: 'I think they are a nice couple. They seem to love him very much already and that puts my mind at rest.' There is a photograph of this meeting in your life story book. At that time Alan was still feeling very angry about the court's decision and didn't feel able to meet them.

Your parents agreed to write to Sally and Alan every year to let them know how you were doing. This was arranged by this authority's confidential letterbox mailing service. Sally also said that she would write back each year with news of her and Alan. I hope this arrangement continued, although it may have been hard for Sally to sustain, as at times her life was pretty chaotic.

By this time you had been living with your foster carers for ten months. You were very attached to your foster carers and they were attached to you. Everyone needed time to get to know each other. Your prospective parents met you on the 18 August 2013 and then came to see you several times at your foster home. Sam then went with you to visit them in their home. After this period of introductions, and when everyone felt that you were ready, you went to live with your mum and dad on 20 September 2013, when you were 11 months old.

I visited you every week for a while and then every month. It was very strange for you at first and you missed your foster carers as you had lived with them for so long. You were clearly a little confused at first. You regressed for a while and needed lots of attention and reassurance. You lost your appetite and you were very unsettled at night. Everything was so new and strange for you, but gradually you settled.

You had your first birthday a month after you moved and you were growing into a gorgeous and lively little boy. You were soon full of life and energy again. You now had more teeth and a big smile to go with those big eyes, and a mass of thick brown curly hair, much like Alan's. Everyone who met you felt that you were just so cute and cuddly. About a month after your first birthday your mum telephoned excitedly to tell me that you had taken your first steps. You could now walk!

We had regular reviews and, when everyone thought that the time was right, about four months after you went to live with them, your mum and dad submitted their application to adopt you. By this time both of your birth parents reluctantly accepted that they were not in a position to look after you and that they could not give you the stability you needed. Sally said that she felt that adoption would be the best thing for you. Alan had also written to me from prison saying that, while he wasn't going to contest the adoption, he didn't feel he could agree with it either.

Eventually, on 20 February 2014 at West London Court, an Adoption Order was made. I attended this hearing and, about a month later on 25 March 2014, you went to court for the Celebratory Hearing with your mum and dad, and your grandparents, Julie and James. I was there as well and Anne from the Adoption Team, so quite a crowd.

You will have seen the photographs of this special day in your Life Story Book. I remember it well. You were wearing your red Christmas jumper – a present from Father Christmas! It had snowflakes and a snowman on it. Your mum said that you loved that jumper and would wear it every day and night if you could. You were growing so fast and they thought that it wouldn't fit you for much longer. As it was your favourite, and a very special jumper, they felt that it was right for this very special day. You didn't really understand the significance, but you know it was an important day. You were very excited and enjoyed running around the court waiting area, playing chasing games with your dad.

We all went into the courtroom to meet the judge. He told you that he was making an Adoption Order and that you would be living with your parents permanently. He gave you a special certificate, showing your new name: Harry James Baker. Your parents added the name James, after your grandfather. Your official new birth and adoption certifications came in the post several weeks later. The judge let you try on his wig and sit in his chair. You loved the huge chair, but you were not so keen on the wig!

We all went to a nearby café after the court hearing and, although it was quite a cold day, you had the most enormous ice cream to celebrate. More than anything else, you were just so excited that you were going home on a train!

I came to see you a week later, partly to check on a few details so that I could finish this letter for you and to say goodbye. You were a little anxious when I first arrived and stayed very close to your mum, but soon relaxed and were your usual cheerful, giggly self. Your mum put some music on and you were soon dancing for me. You clearly had a talent! As I left you were engrossed in one of your favourite films: *Spot the Dog*.

Adoption Support Services

I think that you will have known most of the information in this letter, but seeing it all written down may still be difficult for you, and you may now have some more queries. Your parents may be able to answer any other questions you have or, if you would like to talk to someone else, there is an Adoption Support Service in this authority. The details are at the top of this letter and you can make contact at any time in the future if you would like to clarify any of the information in this letter. If you prefer, you can contact your local Adoption Services wherever you now live, and they will also be able to help you with this.

After the age of 18 years, you could also request access to your adoption records. Again you would need to contact the Adoption

Support Service to organise this. If this is something you would like to do before you are 18 years, then you will have to discuss this with your parents first, so that they can support you with this request.

As I finish this letter you are still only 18 months old. I wonder what you will look like by the time you read this! I imagine that you are a fine looking, tall young man. You will still have those dark eyes and brown hair, but I wonder if you still have those lovely thick curls.

I know that I will think about you over the years and I will smile whenever I remember your energy, your enthusiasm and of course those dance moves! I hope that all has gone well for you and that you had a happy and secure childhood.

I wish you every success and my very best wishes for the future.

Yours sincerely,

Joy Rees
Social Worker
Looked After Children's Team

References

Baynes, P. (2008) 'Untold stories: A discussion of life story work'. *Adoption and Fostering* *32*, 2, 43–49.

Bowlby, J. (1992) *A Secure Base: Clinical Applications of Attachment Theory*. London: Routledge.

Brodzinsky, D.M. and Schechter, M.D. (1990) *The Psychology of Adoption*. New York: Oxford University Press.

Buchanan, A. (2014) 'The Experience of Life Story Work: Reflections of Young People Leaving Care' Unpublished thesis: Cardiff University.

Bunn, A. (2013) 'Signs of Safety in England'. London: NSPCC. Available at www.nspcc.org.uk/services-and-resources/research-and-resources/2013/signs-of-safety-model-england, accessed on 18 September 2017.

Department for Education (2006–2007) *Care Matters Green Paper Consultation*. London: Department for Education.

Department for Education (2010) *IRO Handbook: Statutory Guidance for independent reviewing officers and local authorities on their functions in relation to case management and review for looked after children*. London: Department for Education.

Department for Education (2011) *Fostering Services: National Minimum Standards*. London: Department for Education.

Department for Education (2013) *Adoption: Statutory Guidance*. London: Department for Education.

Department for Education (2014) *Adoption: National Minimum Standards* London: Department for Education.

Department for Education (2016) *Adoption: A Vision for Change* London: Department for Education.

Fahlberg, V. (2003) *A Child's Journey Through Placement*. London: British Agencies for Adoption and Fostering.

Fitzhardinge, H. (2008) 'Adoption, resilience and the importance of stories.' *Adoption and Fostering 7*, 32, 1, 58–64.

Hammond, S.P. and Cooper, N.J. (2013) *Digital Life Story Work: Using Techniques to Help Young People Make Sense of their Experiences.* London: BAAF.

Jensen, F.E. (2015) *Secrets of the Teenage Brain.* London: HarperCollins.

Loxterkamp, L. (2009) 'Contact and truth: The unfolding predicament in adoption and fostering.' *Clinical Child Psychology and Psychiatry, 14,* 3, 423–425.

Moffat, F. (2012) *Writing a Later Life Letter: The Good Practice Guide.* London: BAAF.

Nicholls, E. (2005) *The New Life Work Model: Practice Guide.* Dorset: Russell House Publishing.

Rees, J. (2009) *Life Story Books for Adopted Children: A Family Friendly Approach.* London: Jessica Kingsley Publishers.

Rees J. (2017) *Life Story Books for Adopted and Fostered Children: A Family Friendly Approach.* London: Jessica Kingsley Publishers.

Rose, R. (2012) *Life Story Therapy with Traumatized Children: A Model for Practice.* London: Jessica Kingsley Publishers.

Rose, R. and Philpot, T. (2005) *The Child's Own Story: Life Story Work with Traumatized Children.* London: Jessica Kingsley Publishers.

Ryan, T. and Walker, R. (2016) *Life Story Work: Why, What, How and When.* London: CoramBAAF.

Sayers, A. and Roach, R. (2011) *Child Appreciation Days: Good Practice Guide.* London: BAAF.

SCIE/NICE, (2010) *Recommendations On Looked After Children: Promoting the Quality of Life of Looked After Children and Young People.* London: Social Care Institute of Excellence.

Sydney, L. and Price, E. (2014) *Facilitating Meaningful Contact in Adoption and Fostering: A Trauma-Informed Approach to Planning, Assessing and Good Practice.* London: Jessica Kingsley Publishers.

Tait, A. and Wosu, H. (2013) *Direct Work with Vulnerable Children: Playful Activities and Strategies for Communication.* London: Jessica Kingsley Publishers.

The Urban Child Institute (2017) *Baby's Brain Begins Now: Conception to Age 3.* Available at http://urbanchildinstitute.org, accessed on 1 July 2017.

Triseliotis, J. (1983) 'Identity and security in adoption and long-term fostering.' *Adoption & Fostering, 7,* 1

Triseliotis, J., Shireman, J. and Hundleby, M. (1999). *Adoption theory, policy and practice.* Trowbridge, Wiltshire: Redwood Books.

Verrier, N. (2009) *The Primal Wound: Understanding the Adopted Child.* London: CoramBAAF.

Williams, R. (18 March 2014) Care leavers to get access to their records. *The Guardian.*

Wrench, K. and Naylor, L. (2013) *Life Work with Children Who Are Fostered or Adopted.* London: Jessica Kingsley Publishers.

Suggested reading

Archer, C. (1999) *First Steps in Parenting the Child Who Hurts: Tiddlers and Toddlers*. London: Jessica Kingsley Publishers.

Archer, C. (1999) *Next Steps in Parenting the Child Who Hurts: Tykes and Teens*. London Jessica Kingsley Publishers.

Bowlby, J. (1992) *A Secure Base: Clinical Applications of Attachment Theory* London: Routledge.

Bowlby, J. (2007) *The Making and Breaking of Affectional Bonds*. London: Routledge.

Fahlberg, V. (2003) *A Child's Journey Through Placement*. London: BAAF.

Gerhardt, S. (2004) *Why Love Matters: How Affection Shapes a Baby's Brain*. New York: Routledge.

Golding, K. (2014) *Using Stories to Build Bridges with Traumatized Children: Creative Ideas for Therapy, Life Story Work, Direct Work and Parenting*. London: Jessica Kingsley Publishers.

Hewitt, H. (2006) *Life Story Books for People with Learning Disabilities: A Practical Guide*. Worcester: British Institute of Leaning Disabilities.

Hughes, D. (2007) *Attachment-Focused Family Therapy*. New York: W.W. Norton & Company.

Kranowitz, C.S. (2003) *The Out-of-Sync Child Has Fun: Activities for Kids with Sensory Integration Dysfunction*. New York: Perigee.

Lacher, D., Nichols, T. and May, J. (2005) *Connecting with Kids through Stories: Using Narratives to Facilitate Attachment in Adopted Children*. London: Jessica Kingsley Publishers.

Luckock, B. and Lefevre, M. (2008) *Direct Work: Social Work with Children and Young People in Care*. London: BAAF.

MacLeod, J. and Macrae, S. (2006) *Adoption Parenting: Creating a Toolbox, Building Connections*. New Jersey: EMK Press.

Oaklander, V. (1978) *Windows to Our Children*. New York: Gestalt Journal Press.

Romaine, M., Turley, T. and Tuckey, N. (2007) *Preparing Children for Permanence*. London: BAAF.

Rose, R. and Philpot, T. (2005*) The Child's Own Story: Life Story Work with Traumatized Children*. London: Jessica Kingsley Publishers.

Rosen, S, (1991) *My Voice Will Go With You: The Teaching Tales of Milton H. Erickson*. London: Norton.

Ryan, T. and Walker, R. (2017) *Life Story Work*. London: CoramBAAF.

Siegel, D. and Hartzell, M. (2004) *Parenting from the Inside Out. How a Deeper Self-Inderstanding Can Help You Raise Children Who Thrive*. New York: Penguin.

Silver, M. (2013) *Attachment in Common Sense and Doodles: A Practical Guide*. London: Jessica Kingsley Publishers.

Stringer, B. (2009) *Communicating Through Play: Techniques for Assessing and Preparing Children for Adoption*. London: BAAF.

Sunderland, M. (2004) *Using Story Telling as a Therapeutic Tool with Children*. Oxford: Speechmark Publishing Ltd.

Sunderland, M. (2016) *The Science of Parenting: How Today's Brain Research Can Help You Raise Happy, Emotionally Balanced Children*. London: Dorling Kindersley.

Children's books

Angel, A. (2013) *Adopted Like Me: My Book of Adopted Heroes*. London: Jessica Kingsley Publishers.

Bell, M. (2008) *Elfa and the Box of Memories*. London: BAAF.

Brodzinsky, A. (2013) *Can I Tell You About Adoption?* London: Jessica Kingsley Publishers.

Brodzinsky, A. (2013) *The Mulberry Bird: An Adoption Story*. London: Jessica Kingsley Publishers.

Daniels, R. (2009) *Finding a Family for Tommy*. London: BAAF.

Evans, J. (2014) *How Are You Feeling Today Baby Bear?* London: Jessica Kingsley Publishers.

Foxton, J. (2007) *Spark Learns to Fly*. London: BAAF.

Gliori, D. (2005) *No Matter What*. London: Bloomsbury.

Griffiths, J. and Pilgrim, T. (2007) *Picnic in the Park*. London: BAAF.

Holmes, M.M. (2000) *A Terrible Thing Happened: A Story For Children Who Have Witnessed Violence Or Trauma*. Washington, DC: Magination Press.

Ironside, V. (2015) *The Huge Bag of Worries*. London: Hodder Children's Books.

Janz, M. and Allen, E. (2014) *Why Does Sammy Do That?* UK: Amazon.co.uk.

Levinson Gilman, J. (2002) *Murphy's Three Homes: A Story For Children in Foster Care*. Washington, DC: Magination Press.

MacDonald, A. (1993) *Little Beaver and the Echo*. London: Walker Books.

Naish, S. and Jefferies, R. (2016) *Charley Chatty and the Wiggly Worry Worm*. London: Jessica Kingsley Publishers.

Naish, S. and Jefferies, R. (2016) *Rosie Rudey and the Very Annoying Parent*. London: Jessica Kingsley Publishers.

Naish, S. and Jefferies, R. (2016) *Sophie Spikey Has a Very Big Problem*. London: Jessica Kingsley Publishers.

Naish, S. and Jefferies, R. (2016) *William Wobbly and the Very Bad Day*. London: Jessica Kingsley Publishers.

Parr, T. (2010) *The Family Book*. New York: Little Brown and Company.

Parr, T. (2009) *It's Okay to Be Different.* New York: Little Brown and Company.

Parr, T. (2009) *The Feelings Book.* New York: Little Brown and Company.

Pitcher, D. (2009) *Where is Poppy's Panda?* London: BAAF.

Potter, M. (2014) *How Are Your Feelings Today?* London: Featherstone.

Redford, A. (2016) *The Boy Who Built a Wall Around Himself.* London: Jessica Kingsley Publishers.

Richardson, J. and Parnell, P. (2007) *And Tango Makes Three.* London: Simon and Schuster UK Ltd.

Sambrooks, P. (2013) *Dennis and the Big Decisions.* London: BAAF.

Seeney, J. (2012) *A Safe Place for Rufus.* London: BAAF.

Seeney, J. (2007) *Morris and the Bundle of Worries.* London: BAAF.

Sutherland, M. (2007) Helping Children with Feelings Series: *A Nifflenoo Called Nevermind, Willy and the Wobbly House, The Frog who Longed for the Moon to Smile, The Day the Sea Went Out and Never Came Back, Ruby and the Rubbish Bin, How Hattie Hated Kindness.* Oxford: Speechmark Publishing Ltd.

Sutherland, M. (2012) *Bothered: Helping Teenagers Talk About Their Feelings.* Oxford: Speechmark Publishing Ltd.

Wilgocki, J. and Wright, M.K. (2002) *Maybe Days: A Book For Children in Foster Care.* Washington, DC: Magination Press.